In Their Own Words

"The truth is that all men having power ought to be mistrusted."
—James Madison

"There is nothing wrong in America that can't be fixed with what is right in America."
—William J. Clinton

"An honorable defeat is better than a dishonorable victory."
—Millard Fillmore

"Good ballplayers make good citizens."
—Chester A. Arthur

"If government is to serve any purpose, it is to do for others what they are unable to do for themselves."
—Lyndon B. Johnson

"Liberty, when it begins to take root, is a plant of rapid growth."
—George Washington

"A man is known by the company he keeps, and also by the company from which he is kept out."
—Grover Cleveland

CONTENTS

PART ONE

The Story of the Presidency 4

The Three Branches of Government . . .6

PART TWO

George Washington 8

John Adams 10

Thomas Jefferson 11

James Madison 12

James Monroe 13

John Quincy Adams 14

Andrew Jackson 15

Martin Van Buren 16

William Henry Harrison 17

John Tyler 18

James K. Polk 19

Zachary Taylor 20

Millard Fillmore 21

Franklin Pierce 22

James Buchanan 23

Abraham Lincoln 24

Andrew Johnson 26

Ulysses S. Grant 27

Rutherford B. Hayes 28

James Garfield 29

Chester A. Arthur 30

Grover Cleveland 31

Benjamin Harrison 32

PRESIDENTS
of the United States

By the Editors of TIME For Kids
WITH LISA deMAURO

Collins
An Imprint of HarperCollinsPublishers

About the Author: Lisa deMauro is the author of many books and magazine articles for young people, including the TIME FOR KIDS® Biographies on Theodore Roosevelt and Thomas Edison. She lives in Westchester County, New York, with her husband and two children. The author has been fascinated by the lives of Presidents since she was in elementary school.

Collins is an imprint of HarperCollins Publishers.
Presidents of the United States
Copyright © 2006 by Time Inc.
Used under exclusive license by HarperCollins Publishers Inc.
Manufactured in China.
All rights reserved. No part of this book may be used or reproduced in any manner whatsoever without written permission except in the case of brief quotations embodied in critical articles and reviews. For information address HarperCollins Children's Books, a division of HarperCollins Publishers, 10 East 53rd Street, New York, NY 10022.
www.harpercollinschildrens.com

Library of Congress Cataloging-in-Publication Data is available.

ISBN-10: 0-06-081554-X — ISBN-13: 978-0-06-081554-7
ISBN-10: 0-06-081555-8 (lib. bdg.) — ISBN-13: 978-0-06-081555-4 (lib. bdg.)
ISBN-10: 0-06-081556-6 (pbk.) — ISBN-13: 978-0-06-081556-1 (pbk.)

11 12 13 SCP 10 9 8 7 6
First Edition

J973.099

Copyright © by Time Inc.

TIME FOR KIDS and the Red Border Design are Trademarks of Time Inc. used under license.

Photography and Illustration Credits:
Credits run clockwise from top right of page, except where noted. Cover: center and top right: AP/Wide World Photos, background: see pages 58–61; inside cover flap: David Hume Kennerly/Getty Images; title page: AP/Wide World Photos; p.1: Library of Congress; p.2–3: Library of Congress; Bridwell Library of Southern Methodist University; Paul Schutzer/Time Life Pictures/Getty Images, Library of Congress; p.4–5: Courtesy Winterthur Museum; © New-York Historical Society/Bridgeman Art Library; National Museum of American History/Smithsonian Institution; Robin Miller/Independence National Historic Park; National Museum of American History/Smithsonian Institution; p.7: Digital Stock; p.8–9: © North Wind Picture Archives; Bettmann/Corbis; Bridwell Library of Southern Methodist University; Library of Congress, Art Resource, NY; Comstock; p.10: © Reunion des Musees Nationaux/Art Resource, NY; Bridgeman Art Library/© Massachusetts Historical Society; Library of Congress; Reunion des Musees Nationaux / Art Resource, NY; © North Wind Picture Archives; p.11: Time Picture Collection/Getty Images; Library of Congress; © The New York Public Library/Art Resource, NY; National Archives; p.12: © National Portrait Gallery/Smithsonian Institution/Art Resource, NY; © North Wind Picture Archives; The Granger Collection; Hulton Archive/Getty Images; P.13: Hulton Archive/Getty Images; The Granger Collection; Comstock; ©Superstock, Inc.; The Granger Collection; p.14: Hulton Archive/Getty Images; Mansell Collection/Time Life Pictures/Getty Images; Collection of the New-York Historical Society; Library of Congress; Library of Congress; p.15: Library of Congress; Bridgeman Art Library, The Granger Collection; Library of Congress; p.16: © National Portrait Gallery, Smithsonian Institution/Art Resource, NY; Woolaroc Museum; © Victoria & Albert Museum, London/Art Resource, NY; Library of Congress; p.17: © National Portrait Gallery/Smithsonian Institution/Art Resource, NY; Library of Congress; Time Life Pictures/Getty Images; National Museum of American History/Smithsonian Institution; p.18: © National Portrait Gallery/Smithsonian Institution/Art Resource, NY; Hulton/Getty; Library of Congress; National Library of Medicine; Library of Congress; p.19: Library of Congress; Arne Hodalic/Corbis; Library of Congress; p.20: Bridgeman Art Library/© Chicago Historical Society; Library of Congress; Time Life Pictures/Getty Images; Library of Congress; p.21: Library of Congress; © North Wind Picture Archives; © National Portrait Gallery, Smithsonian Institution/Art Resource, NY; Library of Congress; Library of Congress; p.22: Courtesy Library of Congress; © North Wind Picture Archives; © National Portrait Gallery, Smithsonian Institution/Art Resource, NY; Collection of the New-York Historical Society; p.23: Library of Congress; Library of Congress; © SEF/Art Resource, NY; © North Wind Picture Archives; © National Portrait Gallery/Smithsonian Institution/Art Resource, NY; p.24–25: © National Portrait Gallery, Smithsonian Institution/Art Resource, NY; © Chicago Historical Society/Bridgeman Art Library; Library of Congress; © National Portrait Gallery/Smithsonian Institution/Art Resource, NY; National Archives; © Chicago Historical Society/Bridgeman Art Library; Library of Congress; Library of Congress; p.26: Library of Congress; Library of Congress; Collection of the New-York Historical Society; © North Wind Picture Archives; p.27: Library of Congress; © Smithsonian American Art Museum, Washington, DC/Art Resource, NY; Denver Public Library/Western History Collection; Corbis; Bridwell Library of Southern Methodist University; p.28: Rutherford B. Hayes Presidential Center; Library of Congress; Bettmann/Corbis; Rutherford B. Hayes Presidential Center; p.29: © National Portrait Gallery, Smithsonian Institution/Art Resource, NY; Time Life Pictures/National Archives; Library of Congress; Bettmann/Corbis; p.30: National Archives; Library of Congress; Collection of the New-York Historical Society; Bridgeman Art Library; p.31: Library of Congress; Library of Congress; National Museum of American History/Smithsonian Institution; Library of Congress; National Museum of American History/Smithsonian Institution; p.32: Library of Congress; © The New York Public Library/Art Resource, NY; Corbis; Corbis; Collection of the New-York Historical Society; p.33: Library of Congress; © New York Historical Society/Bridgeman Art Library; Bettmann/Corbis; National Museum of American History/Smithsonian Institution; p.34: Library of Congress; National Archives; © National Portrait Gallery, Smithsonian Institution/Art Resource, NY; Library of Congress; National Museum of American History/Smithsonian Institution; p.35: Hulton Archive/Getty Images; Library of Congress; Library of Congress; National Museum of American History/Smithsonian Institution; p.36: Mansell Collection/Time Life Pictures/Getty Images; Library of Congress; Library of Congress; National Archives; Dr. Thomas J. Knock; p.37: Library of Congress; Library of Congress; Bridwell Library of Southern Methodist University; Hulton Archive/Getty Images; p.38: Library of Congress; Collection of the New-York Historical Society; © National Portrait Gallery/Smithsonian Institution/Art Resource, NY; AP/Wide World Photos; Library of Congress; p.39: Bettmann/Corbis; Bettmann/Corbis; Herbert Hoover Presidential Library and Museum; Collection of the New-York Historical Society; p.40–41: National Archives; Bridwell Library of Southern Methodist University; Franklin D. Roosevelt Library; AP/Wide World Photos; Time Life Pictures/Getty Images; Library of Congress; AP/Wide World Photos; Library of Congress; Hulton Archive/Getty Images; p.42–43: Harry S. Truman Library; National Archives; Harry S. Truman Library; AP/Wide World Photos; Ingram Publishing; Time Life Pictures/Getty Images; AP/Wide World Photos; Library of Congress; Harry S. Truman Library; p.44: Library of Congress; Dwight D. Eisenhower Library and Museum; AP/Wide World Photos; National Archives; p.45: Time Life Pictures/Getty Images; John F. Kennedy Library and Museum; AP/Wide World Photos; AP/Wide World Photos; Time Life Pictures/Getty Images; p.46: Lyndon Baines Johnson Library and Museum; Bill Eppridge/Time Life Pictures/Getty Images; Billy Ray/Time Life Pictures/Getty Images; Lyndon Baines Johnson Library and Museum; Lyndon Baines Johnson Library and Museum; p.47: Corbis/Bettmann; NASA; NASA; Bill Pierce/Time Life Pictures; p.48: Alfred Eisenstaedt/Time Life Pictures/Getty Images; Gerald R. Ford Library; Time Life Pictures; AP/Wide World Photos; AP/Wide World Photos; p.49: © National Portrait Gallery/Smithsonian Institution/Art Resource, NY; Courtesy Rollerblade; AP/Wide World Photos; p.50: Ronald Reagan Presidential Library; NASA; Dirck Halstead/Time Life Pictures/Getty Images; Ronald Reagan Presidential Library; p.51: George Bush Presidential Library; AFP/Getty Images; AP/Wide World Photos; p.52–53: Diana Walker/Time Life Pictures/Getty Images; Cynthia Johnson/Time Life Pictures/Getty Images; AP/Wide World Photos; AP/Wide World Photos; Ron Sachs/Corbis; Cynthia Johnson/Time Life Pictures/Getty Images; Consolidated News Photos/William J. Clinton Library; Time Life Pictures/Getty Images; p.54–55: Time Life Pictures/Getty Images; White House Photos; AP/Wide World Photos; U.S. Marines; European Space Agency; AP/Wide World Photos; AP/Wide World Photos; AP/Wide World Photos; Time Life Pictures/Getty Images; p.56–57: © New-York Historical Society/Bridgeman Art Library; Lyndon Baines Johnson Library and Museum; AP/Wide World Photos; Time Life Pictures/Getty Images; Library of Congress; Hulton Archive/Getty Images; Courtesy of the Mount Vernon Ladies Association; p.58–59: Christie's Images/Corbis (Washington); John Trumbull/National Portrait Gallery/Smithsonian Institution (Adams); Mather Brown/National Portrait Gallery/Smithsonian Institution, bequest of Charles Francis Adams (Jefferson); Chester Harding/National Portrait Gallery/Smithsonian Institution (Madison); John Vanderlyn, National Portrait Gallery/Smithsonian Institution (Monroe); George Caleb Bingham/National Portrait Gallery/Smithsonian Institution (J.Q. Adams); Ralph Eleaser Whiteside Earl/National Portrait Gallery/Smithsonian Institution, gift of Andrew W. Mellon (Jackson); Mathew B. Brady/National Portrait Gallery/Smithsonian Institution (Van Buren); Albert Gallatin Hoit/National Portrait Gallery/Smithsonian Institution (Harrison); Library of Congress (Tyler); Max Westfield/National Portrait Gallery/Smithsonian Institution (Polk); James Reid Lambdin/National Portrait Gallery/Smithsonian Institution, gift of Barry Bingham Sr. (Taylor); National Portrait Gallery/Smithsonian Institution (Fillmore); George Peter Healy/National Portrait Gallery/Smithsonian Institution, gift of Andrew W. Mellon (Pierce); George Peter Healy/National Portrait Gallery/Smithsonian Institution, gift of Andrew W. Mellon (Buchanan); George Peter Healy/National Portrait Gallery/Smithsonian Institution (Lincoln); Washington Bogart Cooper/National Portrait Gallery/Smithsonian Institution (Johnson); Thomas Le Clear/National Portrait Gallery/Smithsonian Institution, gift of Mrs. Grant (Grant); p.60–61: Bettmann/Corbis (Hayes); Ole Peter Hansen Balling/National Portrait Gallery/Smithsonian Institution, gift of IBM (Garfield); Ole Peter Hansen Balling/National Portrait Gallery/Smithsonian Institution, gift of Mrs. H.N. Blue (Arthur); Anders Zorn/National Portrait Gallery/Smithsonian Institution (Cleveland); Library of Congress (Harrison); Adolfo Muller; Ury/National Portrait Gallery/Smithsonian Institution (McKinley); Adrian Lamb/National Portrait Gallery/Smithsonian Institution, gift of T.R. Assoc. (Roosevelt); William Valentine Schevill/National Portrait Gallery/Smithsonian Institution, gift of W.E. Schevill (Taft); Edmund Tarbell/National Portrait Gallery/Smithsonian Institution (Wilson); Margaret Lindsay Williams/NPG/SI (Harding); Joseph E. Burgess/Mellon Bruce (Eisenhower); JFK Presidential Library (Kennedy); Peter Hurd/National Portrait Gallery/Smithsonian Institution, gift of Phi Gamma Delta (Coolidge); Douglas Chandor/National Portrait Gallery/Smithsonian Institution (Hoover); Oscar White/Corbis (FDR); Greta Kempton/National Portrait Gallery/Smithsonian Institution (Truman); Thomas Edgar Stephens/National Portrait Gallery/Smithsonian Institution, gift of Ailsa Mellon Bruce (Eisenhower); JFK Presidential Library (Kennedy); Peter Hurd/National Portrait Gallery/Smithsonian Institution, gift of the artist (Johnson); Norman Rockwell/National Portrait Gallery/Smithsonian Institution, gift of Nixon Foundation (Nixon); Everett R. Kinstler/National Portrait Gallery/Smithsonian Institution, gift of Ford Foundation (Ford); Jimmy Carter Presidential Library (Carter); Ronald Reagan Presidential Library (Reagan); Ronald N. Sherr/National Portrait Gallery/Smithsonian Institution, George Bush Presidental Library (Bush); Bettmann/Corbis (Clinton); Eric Draper/White House (G.W. Bush); p.62–63: John Roman for TIME FOR KIDS; Photos.com Select/Index Open; p.64: Colleen Pidel; Digital Stock; AP/Wide World Photos; p.65 all: Digital Stock; p.66: National Archives; Ingram Publishing; Photodisc; p. 70: Library of Congress; back cover: AP/Wide World Photos; Rutherford B. Hayes Presidential Center; Lyndon Baines Johnson Library and Museum; Franklin D. Roosevelt Library; Collection of the New-York Historical Society.

Acknowledgments:
For TIME FOR KIDS: Editorial Director: Keith Garton; Contributors: Jonathan Rosenbloom, Elizabeth Winchester; Indexer: Marilyn Rowland; Art Director: Rachel Smith; Designer: Colleen Pidel; Photography Editors: Alan Gottlieb, Angelique Sieniawski

HarperCollins books may be purchased for educational, business, or sales promotional use. For information, please write: Special Markets Department, HarperCollins Publishers Inc., 10 East 53rd Street, New York, NY 10022.

go **Stay on top of presidential politics at www.timeforkids.com**

William McKinley 33

Theodore Roosevelt 34

William H. Taft 35

Woodrow Wilson 36

Warren G. Harding 37

Calvin Coolidge 38

Herbert Hoover 39

Franklin D. Roosevelt 40

Harry S. Truman 42

Dwight D. Eisenhower 44

John F. Kennedy 45

Lyndon B. Johnson 46

Richard M. Nixon 47

Gerald R. Ford 48

Jimmy Carter 49

Ronald W. Reagan 50

George H. W. Bush 51

William J. Clinton 52

George W. Bush 54

PART THREE

The Nation's First Ladies 56

Presidents at a Glance 58

Welcome to the White House 62

Postcards from Washington, D.C. 64

Presidents by the Numbers 66

Index 67

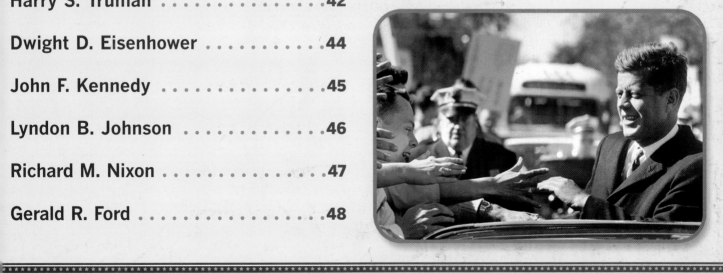

The Story of the Presidency

n 1787 America's founding fathers faced an enormous task. They had to create a strong government for the new country. Representatives from each of the states, called delegates, met in Philadelphia. General George Washington was asked to lead the meeting we now call the Constitutional Convention. He had directed the military during the country's successful war for independence from Great Britain. And he

▶ Federal Hall in New York City was home to the new nation's government.

FEDERAL HALL
The Seat of CONGRESS.

was the new nation's first great hero.

The war had ended four years earlier. During that time the former colonies were governed by the Articles of Confederation. This document provided direction to the new states but only loosely tied them together as a nation. The delegates made a plan for the nation's government and its citizens by writing the U.S. Constitution.

Leading a Nation

The delegates had different ideas about the job and powers of the country's leader. They had not liked being ruled by England's strong king. Some people even argued that America should have several top leaders, not just one, to make sure that the leader did not become as powerful as a king. While the delegates finally agreed to have one person head the nation, they made sure to create a system that

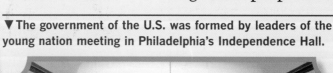

▼ The government of the U.S. was formed by leaders of the young nation meeting in Philadelphia's Independence Hall.

▲ Washington's officer's uniform, battle sword, and sheath from the 1790s are shown.

▲ On April 30, 1789, Washington stood on the balcony of Federal Hall in New York City and recited the presidential oath of office. This engraving is the only known depiction of Washington's first inauguration from the period.

would check, or control, the power of the leader. (See page 6.)

The delegates also struggled with how long the leader should serve. Some felt one long term, of up to seven years, would be best. Because the leader wouldn't be allowed to run for reelection, he wouldn't be concerned with winning support from voters while he was in charge of the country. Others felt short terms would be better. The delegates came to agree that the leader could serve a term of four years and could run for reelection when the term ended.

A Powerful Position

By the end of the convention, the delegates had outlined the powers of the nation's top leader. These powers include serving as the head of the military, making agreements with other nations, and choosing people to hold important government jobs. In 1788 the method of election was different in every state. In some states the public voted, and in others the state lawmakers voted. But people sent to represent the states, called the electoral college, cast the final votes.

On April 30, 1789, George Washington became the first person to be elected to this powerful position. After the election people debated what to call Washington. Some ideas were "His Elective Majesty" and even "His Highness, the President of the United States and Protector of the Rights of the Same." The final decision was to use the simple title "President of the United States." ✪

► The documents from the 1787 Constitutional Convention were kept in this trunk.

The Three Branches of Government

The writers of the Constitution wanted to create a very strong national government. But they also wanted to make sure that one person or group did not have too much power. Their solution was to separate the government's powers into three parts called the legislative, executive, and judicial branches. Each branch of government can limit the powers of the others. This way no branch becomes too powerful. ✪

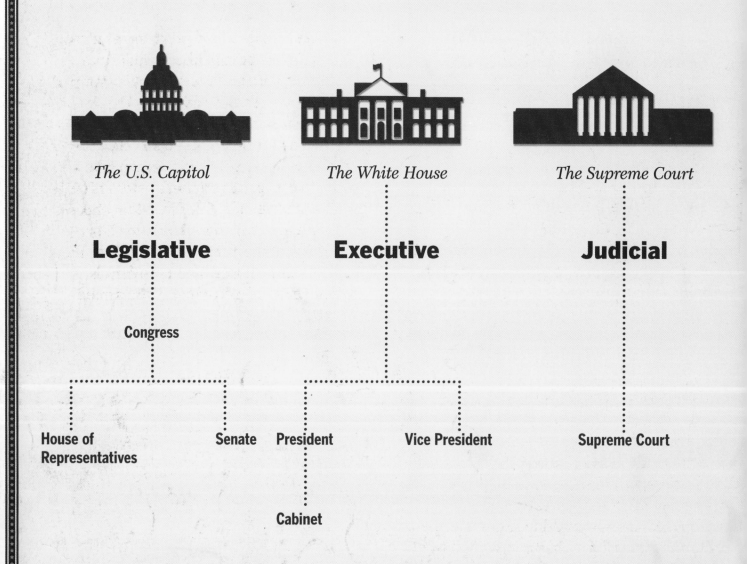

The U.S. Capitol　　　*The White House*　　　*The Supreme Court*

Legislative　　　**Executive**　　　**Judicial**

Congress

House of Representatives　　　Senate　　　President　　　Vice President　　　Supreme Court

Cabinet

Legislative ▶

The legislative branch includes the two houses of Congress—the Senate and the House of Representatives. There are 100 senators and 435 congressmen and congresswomen, the terms used to identify members of the House. They write bills and then vote on whether or not the bills should become laws. Other jobs include deciding how the federal budget will be spent. The legislative branch also must vote before the U.S. may go to war with another country. Senators serve in office for six-year terms. Members of the House of Representatives serve for two-year terms. ✪

The U.S. Capitol

The White House

◀ Executive

The President is head of the executive branch. This branch also includes the vice president and the cabinet, a group of the President's close advisors. The President signs bills to turn them into laws. The President may also veto, or reject, bills. But Congress can take a vote to cancel a President's veto. This is called an override. The President chooses cabinet members and Supreme Court judges, but the Senate must approve the President's choices. The President is also commander-in-chief of the armed forces. ✪

Judicial ▶

The Supreme Court is the head of the judicial branch. It is the most powerful court in the country. Its nine justices, or judges, decide if laws agree with the Constitution. Once justices are approved to serve on the Supreme Court, they can stay on the court for the rest of their lives. ✪

The Supreme Court

7

George Washington

1st *President* ★ 1789-1797

▶ General Washington led the colonial army to victory over the British.

George Washington is called the "father of our country." No one deserves that title more than this well-respected hero of the American Revolution.

Washington came from a successful farming family in Virginia. As a young man, he was happy being a plantation owner and surveyor. He served with the British army during the French and Indian Wars. He also served in Virginia's colonial government.

It was a time of change in Britain's American colonies.

◀ Washington was one of the best horsemen of his time.

Did You Know?

Washington's farewell speech is still read aloud in both houses of Congress every year.

During the 1770s, the colonists were upset that the British made them pay large taxes on goods sent to the colonies. They felt they had no voice in Britain and were being taxed unfairly. Starting in 1775, leaders from the thirteen colonies met in Philadelphia to talk about what to do. George Washington was there at the First and Second Continental Congresses. When a colonial army was formed to fight the British, Washington was selected to take command. In the eyes of King George III and the British, he was now a traitor.

A year later, when the colonial congress adopted a Declaration of Independence from Britain, Washington was in charge of the army of the new United States. His army wasn't well trained. His soldiers didn't have enough supplies. But Washington was a smart leader. And the new nation's army got help from the French. The French were happy to fight against their enemy, Britain.

In 1781 the British lost an important battle at Yorktown, Virginia. Then in April 1783 the Americans won their freedom

KEY DATES

1789 ▶ French Revolution begins.

1790 U.S. Supreme Court meets for the first time. First U.S. census counts nearly four million people.

1791 First ten amendments to the Constitution are approved (Bill of Rights).

when the British gave up all claims to the former colonies.

General Washington returned to a quiet life at Mount Vernon. But Washington's quiet life didn't last long.

After the war the new United States of America was held together by weak laws called the Articles of Confederation. A meeting was held in Philadelphia in 1787 to create a new Constitution. This would be a plan that would include a strong central government to help the states work together. Washington attended and was elected president of this meeting. And in June 1788 the new Constitution was approved by the states and became the foundation of American government.

When it was time to choose a leader of the new government, Washington was the one man everyone trusted. He was elected President of the new nation. In a world of kings and queens, Washington proved that a President chosen by the people could be a strong leader. He showed that the states would have to listen to the federal government. And after two terms, he showed that leadership could pass on peacefully. He died two years later. Congressman Henry Lee said he was "first in war, first in peace, and first in the hearts of his countrymen." ✪

► The President and his first cabinet. Left to right: Washington, Henry Knox, Alexander Hamilton, Thomas Jefferson, and Edmund Randolph

► Brass buttons were worn at Washington's inauguration.

◄ **1793** Eli Whitney invents the cotton gin, or engine.

1794 Slavery is abolished in the French colonies.

1795 Metric system is introduced in France.

John Adams

► Adams proved the nation could survive a change in leaders.

John Adams was used to being in the thick of the action. As a young lawyer in Massachusetts, he became a leader in the fight for America's independence. He attended the Continental Congresses. He worked with Thomas Jefferson on the wording of the Declaration of Independence. He served as a diplomat for the colonies in Europe. And then he became the country's first vice president. He described the position as an "insignificant office" because he did not have enough to do.

Did You Know?

Adams established the U.S. Navy and ordered the first warships to be built.

In 1796 Adams beat Thomas Jefferson in the race for President. Like Washington before him, Adams wanted to keep the U.S. from taking sides in a war between France and Britain. Those countries were fighting, and American shipping was suffering as a result.

When the French attacked U.S. ships, Adams sent diplomats to France for peace talks. Three French officials told the Americans that there would be no talks until the U.S. paid a lot of money to France. When this story got out, many angry Americans wanted war. The French officials were known as X, Y, and Z, so the scandal became known as the XYZ Affair.

In 1800 Adams sent more diplomats to France. This time they were successful and a peace treaty was signed. Adams was proud that he had kept the U.S. out of war. He ran again for President that year, but this time Jefferson won.

As time passed, Adams and his rival Jefferson became close friends. Adams died on July 4, 1826, just hours after Jefferson died in Virginia. ✪

▼ Adams's wife, Abigail, was his most important advisor.

KEY DATES

1798 ▶
Napoleon conquers Rome and Egypt for France.

1800 ▶
The U.S. capital is moved from Philadelphia to Washington, DC.

1801 United Kingdom of Great Britain and Ireland is established with one monarch and one parliament.

Thomas Jefferson

3rd *President* ★ *1801-1809*

Thomas Jefferson grew up in a wealthy plantation family. Taught by private tutors, his education was better than most in the mid-1700s. He was a great thinker, architect, inventor, farmer, and patriot. Tall and with a face full of freckles, Jefferson was more comfortable writing his thoughts than speaking in public. So when it came time for the colonies to break away from Britain, Jefferson was asked to write the Declaration of Independence.

After the Revolutionary War, when the colonies became free, Jefferson was America's ambassador to France. After several years Jefferson wanted to return to Monticello, his Virginia home, to write and farm. But when George Washington became President, he asked Jefferson to be secretary of state—the person in charge of dealing with foreign nations.

The country continued to need him, so in 1796 Jefferson was elected vice president. Four years later he beat John Adams to become President. During his first term, Jefferson made an important decision. In 1803 he bought a huge area of land from France. The Louisiana Purchase just about doubled the size of the nation. Jefferson sent Meriwether Lewis and William Clark to explore the new territory. The men, along with others on their team, went all the way to the Pacific coast! The group returned in 1806 with important information about the areas in the western part of the continent.

After two terms as President, Jefferson went back to Monticello. He helped start up the University of Virginia in 1819. And he continued to write until his death on July 4, 1826—fifty years after he wrote the Declaration of Independence. ✪

Did You Know?

It was Jefferson's idea to create U.S. money on a decimal system with the dollar, or 100 cents, as the base.

▶ Benjamin Franklin and John Adams helped Jefferson write the Declaration of Independence.

KEY DATES

1804 Haiti becomes the first black nation to break free from European rule when it gets its independence from France.

1807 ▶ Robert Fulton makes the first steamboat trip, going from New York City to Albany, NY.

1808 Beethoven's *Fifth* and *Sixth Symphonies* are performed for the first time.

James Madison

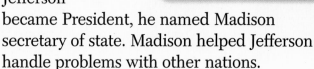

James Madison, the son of a Virginia plantation owner, was a small man who was often sick. He felt that he was too weak to hold an important job. But Madison was a strong thinker and an expert on British laws. When the American colonies finally broke away from Britain, Madison knew that the new country would need a new government. He wanted it to be strong enough to protect people's rights, but not so strong that it could take away people's freedom.

▲ Madison was only thirty-six when he wrote the Bill of Rights.

The U.S. needed a written plan so all the people would know the laws. Madison was just the person to help. He wrote many parts of the new U.S. Constitution, including what became the Bill of Rights. Then he did something even more difficult: He helped convince people to accept it.

One of Madison's closest friends was Thomas Jefferson. When Jefferson became President, he named Madison secretary of state. Madison helped Jefferson handle problems with other nations.

When Madison was elected President, France and Britain were still fighting a war. The U.S. was caught in the middle. When the British attacked American ships, Madison felt it was time to fight back. The War of 1812 lasted about two years. In the end the war was seen as an American victory and Madison left office as a popular President.

In 1817 he went back to his Virginia farm. For the rest of his life, he thought and wrote about the best ways for people and countries to get along with one another. ✪

Did You Know?

In 1814 British forces invaded Washington, D.C., and set fire to the White House.

KEY DATES

1811 The largest series of earthquakes known in North America happen in Mississippi River valley.

1812 Napoleon, emperor of France, invades Russia and loses 600,000 soldiers.

◄ **1814** Francis Scott Key writes "The Star-Spangled Banner" as he watches British attack on Fort McHenry.

James Monroe

5th *President* ★ 1817-1825

▲ President Monroe, at globe, discusses the independence of North and South American nations with his cabinet.

James Monroe was a Virginia college student in 1776 in the early days of the American Revolution. He wanted to help, so he joined Washington's army.

When Thomas Jefferson was President, he sent Monroe to France to discuss the territory called Louisiana. This was a huge piece of land in North America that the French controlled. Monroe helped Jefferson buy the land in the Louisiana Purchase.

Monroe had many friends in government. He had been governor of Virginia, a U.S. senator, and a diplomat to Britain and to France. Monroe served as Madison's secretary of state and secretary of war. When he ran for President, he won easily.

While Monroe was President, more changes to the U.S. took place. On the western edge of the nation, Missouri wanted to enter the union as a slave state. Some people didn't want any more slave states. Finally in 1820 an agreement was reached, called the Missouri Compromise. It allowed Maine to enter as a new free state and Missouri to enter as a slave state. It also said there couldn't be any more slave states north of Missouri.

In 1819 Monroe agreed to purchase Florida from Spain. Then in 1823 he made a very important speech. He said that the countries of Europe must keep out of the affairs of the independent nations and colonies in North and South America. This idea became known as the Monroe Doctrine.

At the end of two terms, Monroe went home to Virginia. This hardworking President helped the U.S. grow in size and power. ✪

Did You Know?

Monroe was the first President to go without wearing a wig in formal public appearances.

▲ The Louisiana Purchase doubled the size of the U.S. territory.

KEY DATES

1819 Simón ▶ Bolívar leads wars for independence throughout South America.

1821 ▶ Mexico declares independence from Spain.

1825 First passenger-carrying railroad opens in England.

John Quincy Adams

6th *President* ★ 1825-1829

It's not surprising that John Quincy Adams was interested in public service. As the son of the second President, he got a close look at the life of a political leader and diplomat. He ended up being both.

Adams was seven when the American Revolution began. As a teenager he left Massachusetts and traveled with his father, who was representing the new U.S. to governments in Europe. Young Adams was a diplomat in Europe himself during the French Revolution in 1789. He returned to France as the U.S. ambassador from 1809 until 1817.

His time in Europe helped Adams form strong opinions about the role the U.S. should play in the world. Adams had seen how nations could pull each other into war. He thought the U.S. should never take the side of one nation over the other.

When James Monroe became President, Adams was his secretary of state. In 1824 Adams ran for President. Andrew Jackson got more of the votes, but neither candidate got enough electoral votes. The House of Representatives had to pick a winner. They chose Adams.

Jackson complained that the election had been unfair. There was no proof of this, but the charge made things hard for President Adams.

In the next election, Jackson beat Adams. Rather than giving up, Adams later ran for a lower office. He became a representative in Congress, where he spoke out against slavery. He also helped create the museum and study center called the Smithsonian Institution. Adams is often said to have been the smartest man to ever hold the office of President. He served in Congress until his death in 1848. ✪

Did You Know?

As President, John Quincy Adams owned a pet alligator that he kept in the White House.

◄ This box was used in John Quincy Adams's presidential campaign as free advertising.

KEY DATES

1827 First ▶ black newspaper, *Freedom's Journal,* begins publishing.

1828 Construction begins on the first public railroad in the U.S. (B&O Railroad).

1829 At the age ▶ of twenty, Louis Braille develops a system of six dots to help the blind read.

14

Andrew Jackson

7th *President* ★ *1829-1837*

On the day Andrew Jackson took office, a newspaper wrote, "It was a proud day for the people. General Jackson is their own president." Americans thought Jackson was a common man partly because of his background. He was born in a log cabin. His father died before he was born and his mother died when he was fourteen. He didn't have a lot of formal schooling.

As a young man, Jackson studied law and made money trading furs and crops. Later he bought a plantation and slaves in Tennessee. But Jackson was still known as a man of the people because he didn't trust the rich, educated class. He believed that common citizens should run the country. He thought government should be simple and straightforward so that anyone could serve.

▲ General Jackson earned the nickname Old Hickory for his toughness.

During the War of 1812, Jackson was a major general. He led his men to a victory against the British at New Orleans. After that, Jackson was a hero. He ran for President in 1824 and got more votes than John Quincy Adams. But Adams won more electoral college votes. In 1828 Jackson ran again and beat Adams.

Jackson was a powerful President. He fought with Congress and disagreed with laws they tried to pass that he thought favored the wealthy. Some people thought he was too strong. They called him King Andrew.

After two terms as President, Jackson spent the rest of his life at the Hermitage, his Tennessee home. He couldn't simply rest. So he gave advice to the new President, Martin Van Buren. Jackson wanted to be sure his policies continued. ✪

Did You Know?

Jackson's enemies called him a jackass (donkey), and Jackson decided to use the animal on his campaign posters. Ever since, the donkey has been the Democrats' symbol.

KEY DATES

1830 Jackson signs the Indian Removal Act, which says Native Americans must leave their homes and move west to the frontier.

1833 The world's first train wreck in New Jersey kills two and injures all others. Former President John Quincy Adams is on board.

◄ **1836** Texas declares independence from Mexico. The Mexican army wins battle at the Alamo. Texas army wins battle at San Jacinto and the war.

Martin Van Buren

eople called Martin Van Buren the Little Magician, but not because he could make a rabbit disappear. Van Buren's magic was political. He was a friendly, cheerful person who knew how to work with people and how to get things done.

Van Buren was born in 1782 in Kinderhook, New York. He is the first President who did not start life as a British subject. His father owned a tavern where people met to talk, so Van Buren heard a lot about politics as a child.

As a teen Van Buren learned about law by working for an attorney. Later, as a New York City lawyer, he met people who were involved in politics.

Van Buren held many offices over the years. He was a state senator, a U.S. senator, and New York's governor. Along the way, Van Buren became

▲ The President in 1838

a big supporter of Andrew Jackson.

When Jackson became President, Van Buren was his secretary of state. He was vice president during Jackson's second term. With Jackson's support, Van Buren was elected President in 1836. But there was some big trouble waiting for him.

As President, Jackson had put the Bank of the United States out of business. That started a chain reaction. Shortly after Van Buren became President, banks all over the country started failing. Many people lost jobs. Voters blamed the new President for the bad times. When Van Buren tried to run again, he lost.

Van Buren hoped to be reelected someday. He ran again in 1848 and lost. People still blamed him for the big economic depression. He spent his retirement years quietly at home in Kinderhook. ✪

◄ As governor of New York, Van Buren gave jobs to his supporters. This was known as the "spoils system."

Did You Know?

The ancestors of Van Buren and his wife were from Holland, and he and the First Lady spoke Dutch at home.

KEY DATES

◄ **1837** Victoria becomes queen of Great Britain.

1838 Over 15,000 ► Cherokees are forced to walk from Georgia to Indian Territory. About 4,000 die along the Trail of Tears.

1839 West African slaves take control of the Cuban slave ship *Amistad*.

William Henry Harrison

▲ An 1840 campaign banner

What most people remember about William Henry Harrison is his campaign slogan and how short his time as President was. Like many of the earlier Presidents, Harrison was from Virginia. He began studying to be a doctor, but when his father died, he left his studies and joined the army to earn a living. For the rest of his life, he divided his time between the army and politics.

In the early 1800s many Indians were being forced off their land to make way for white settlers. Harrison made a big name for himself fighting Indians. In 1811 he won a battle against the Shawnee in Indiana, near a river called Tippecanoe. From that battle he got the nickname Tippecanoe. Later Harrison fought and won an important battle against the British and their Indian partners in the War of 1812.

As a war hero, Harrison was popular with voters. After he settled in Ohio, he became a state senator, a U.S. congressman, a U.S. senator, and the ambassador to Colombia, South America.

Harrison ran for President against Martin Van Buren in 1836. He lost, but in 1840 he ran again. His running mate was named John Tyler. They had a popular slogan: Tippecanoe and Tyler, too.

Harrison took office on a cold, wet day in March 1841. Despite the weather, Harrison gave a long speech outdoors. Soon after, he became seriously ill with pneumonia. He died just thirty-one days after his inauguration. He was the first President to die while in office. ✪

Did You Know?
Harrison was the first presidential candidate to campaign for himself.

▲ General Harrison became a hero at the battle of Tippecanoe in 1811.

KEY DATES

1841 Twenty-six states make up the U.S. and the population reaches seventeen million.

◄ **1841** Adolphe Sax invents the saxophone in Belgium.

1841 Explorer James Ross discovers the deepest bay in Antarctica, now called the Ross Sea.

John Tyler

The U.S. Constitution says that if the President dies, "the powers and duties of [the] office…shall [pass to] the Vice President." But what does that mean? Does the former vice president get all the power of an elected leader? Or is he an "acting President," just carrying on the plans of the old President?

When President Harrison died, these questions had to be answered for the first time. Harrison's vice president, John Tyler, was ready to take over. "I am the President," he said, adding that no one could tell him what to do.

Tyler was from a wealthy Virginia family. He had been a U.S. congressman, a governor, and a U.S. senator. He had experience in office and felt he was ready to lead the country.

Tyler had been picked to run for vice president because he was popular with southern voters. But no one expected him to be in charge of the whole country.

Many congressmen made it difficult for President Tyler. They worked against him. They even threw him out of the Whig Party, which made it hard to run for election in 1844!

But Tyler kept working on things he believed in. He worked to make it easier for settlers to get land in the West. Tyler also got approval from Congress to claim Texas for the U.S. He hoped his actions would lead to the spread of slavery in the new territories.

When the Civil War began sixteen years later, Tyler was elected to be a member of the Confederate Congress. Because of this, Tyler is the only President ever to be named an enemy of the U.S. ✪

◀ Tyler died at home in Virginia before he took office in the Confederate Congress.

Did You Know?

Tyler was the first President to lose his wife while in office and the first to marry while in office.

KEY DATES

▶ **1842** Ether is used in surgery for first time to eliminate pain.

1843 Charles Dickens publishes *A Christmas Carol.*

1844 ▶ Samuel Morse patents the telegraph.

18

James K. Polk

11th *President* ★ *1845-1849*

▶ James Polk was the first President to be photographed while in office (February 1849).

When James Knox Polk first ran for President, his opponent asked, "Who is James K. Polk?" Polk wasn't really unknown, but it was a surprise that he was running for the nation's highest office.

Polk was born in North Carolina. He became a lawyer in Tennessee and also served in state government. Then he became a U.S. congressman and, later, governor of Tennessee.

Polk got to be a presidential candidate because of his views on Texas. The other people who were hoping to run for President in 1844 didn't want to give their opinions on letting Texas into the Union. Texas would have been a slave state, which would make northern voters unhappy. Polk wanted Texas in the Union. So to

Did You Know?
The election on Nov. 7, 1844, was the first time the election for President was held on the same day across the U.S.

satisfy Northerners, he proposed taking the Oregon Territory in the West from Britain. Oregon would then be a free territory.

Polk was a strong leader. In 1846 he sent troops to Texas because of a disagreement over the borders. This led to war with Mexico. It cost thousands of lives but ended in the U.S. getting territory that went from New Mexico to California. He also got Britain to agree that the U.S. would own Oregon Territory, the land that includes Oregon, Idaho, Washington, and parts of Montana and Wyoming. Polk had delivered on his campaign promises.

Polk was very popular and he had enough support in Congress to get a solution agreed to on the issue of slavery. But even though he had greatly expanded U.S. territory, he never made a decision about whether the new territories would allow slavery. This caused even more tensions between North and South. ✪

▲ When the war with Mexico ended, the U.S. had gained about half the land belonging to Mexico.

KEY DATES

1845 Edgar Allan Poe publishes *The Raven and Other Poems*. Knickerbocker Club establishes game rules for baseball.

1846 War declared against Mexico. Failure of potato crop causes famine in Ireland.

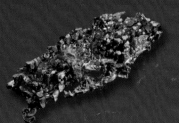

◀**1848** Gold is discovered at Sutter's Mill in California. War with Mexico ends.

Zachary Taylor

Zachary Taylor wasn't a political person. He had never worked in government. He didn't even vote in elections. When his name came up as a presidential candidate, he thought it was a strange idea. But Taylor was a national hero and the public loved him.

Taylor was born in a log cabin in Virginia. He grew up in the frontier outpost of Kentucky. Unlike most Presidents, he never studied law. Taylor was always a soldier. He fought in the War of 1812 and in many battles against Indian tribes. Taylor was also known for forcing whites to obey treaties that protected Indian land. But it was his success in battles against Mexico that made him a hero.

During his war years, Taylor's men gave him the nickname Old Rough and Ready, because he was

▶ War hero Taylor was the first President who had never held a political office.

tough. He shared the hardships of his soldiers. Taylor was not a proud man. He usually didn't wear a uniform. His clothes were often worn and dirty.

As President, Taylor did things his own way. He was a slave owner who was ready to go to war to keep the Union together. He said he would hang any Southerners who would try to break away from the Union. There were thirty states, equally split between slave and free states. When Taylor urged Congress to admit California and New Mexico to the Union as free states, Southerners felt he had turned against them.

In 1850 President Taylor became ill after a long day of Fourth of July speeches. He died a few days later. Taylor's difficult presidency lasted only sixteen months. ✪

Did You Know?

Taylor was so sloppy as President that people seeing him on the streets of Washington often didn't know that the crumpled gentleman was President.

▶ This tobacco tin carries Taylor's image and nickname.

GREENE. T. PACE
ROUGH & READY
TWIST
DANVILLE, VA.

KEY DATES

1849 The Gold Rush begins as thousands head to California seeking fortunes from gold.

▶ **1849** Elizabeth Blackwell of New York becomes first woman doctor.

1850 New census shows 23.1 million people live in U.S. plus 3.2 million enslaved African Americans.

Millard Fillmore

▲ A Whig Party banner from the 1848 election

Millard Fillmore became President upon the death of Zachary Taylor. But no one who knew Fillmore in his childhood could ever have imagined he would be the leader of the nation.

Born into a very poor farm family in New York, Fillmore had less than one year of education. He worked every day as a child on the farm. When he became a teen, he trained to be a cloth maker. But Fillmore wanted to learn to read and write. Soon he found a tutor, Abigail, whom he later married.

Before his election as Taylor's vice president, Fillmore had been elected to the New York state government and was a U.S. congressman. When he became vice president, he and President Taylor didn't agree on much. Taylor was angry at threats from southern states to leave the united nation. Fillmore wanted to keep the Southerners happy.

Once Fillmore became President, he quickly moved to support laws to let California enter the Union as a free state but allow slavery in the new territories in the Southwest. In addition, enslaved people who escaped to free territory could be caught and returned to slavery under the plan. These laws, called the Compromise of 1850, didn't please anyone in the North or the South. But they probably helped delay the start of the Civil War.

At the next election in 1852, the Whig Party, which had chosen him as vice president, would not support him for President. Fillmore ran unsuccessfully for President again in 1856. He then gave up politics and spent the rest of his life back home in Buffalo, New York. ✪

▼ Fillmore's friend Senator Henry Clay argues for the Compromise of 1850 in front of the U.S. Senate.

Did You Know?

First Lady Abigail Powers Fillmore was a teacher who had the first library installed in the White House.

KEY DATES

1850 California becomes the thirty-first state; joins U.S. as a free state.

◀**1852** Author Harriet Beecher Stowe publishes *Uncle Tom's Cabin*, supporting the antislavery movement.

◀**1853** Fillmore sends Commodore Matthew Perry to Japan to open trade with the nation.

Franklin Pierce

14th *President* ★ *1853-1857*

Franklin Pierce once said that he felt being President was "an impossible task to undertake in one term." But he never got the chance to see what two terms would bring.

▲ An 1852 campaign medal for General Pierce

Born and raised in New Hampshire, Pierce practiced law as a young man. Then he served in his state's government and in the U.S. Congress in both houses. In 1842 he decided to give up politics to please his wife, Jane, who disliked Washington, D.C. Four years later Pierce went to fight in the Mexican War. After the war he returned to his law practice and continued speaking about national issues.

As the 1852 presidential election drew close, the Democrats couldn't agree on a candidate. They chose Pierce, thinking a pro-slavery Northerner would appeal to most voters. They were right.

Soon after Pierce won the election, things began to go wrong. In early 1853, Pierce's only living son was killed in a train accident. The First Lady was so upset that she would not appear in public for months. Soon after the inauguration, the vice president, William R. King, died of tuberculosis. The President began his term as a sad, tired man.

Pierce signed into law the Kansas-Nebraska Act, which undid the antislavery part of the Missouri Compromise of 1820. The act said that settlers in Kansas and Nebraska could choose whether or not to allow slavery. People for and against slavery fought for control of Kansas, which became known as Bleeding Kansas.

As Pierce's term ended, the Democratic Party wouldn't support his reelection. He returned to New Hampshire with the divided nation ever closer to civil war. ✪

▶ The bloody war over slavery in Kansas cost Pierce a second term.

Did You Know?

Pierce was the first President to have hot and cold running water in the White House.

KEY DATES

1853 Yellow fever kills 7,790 people in New Orleans.

1854 Republican Party ▶ is formed by antislavery Northerners. Henry David Thoreau publishes *Walden*.

1855 Florence Nightingale nurses the wounded in the Crimean War (Ukraine).

James Buchanan

15th *President* ★ *1857-1861*

James Buchanan was elected President of a country in conflict. Northerners wanted to stop slavery from spreading to new parts of the country. Some, called abolitionists, wanted to end slavery completely. Southerners wanted new states and territories to be able to choose whether to allow slavery.

Buchanan's term began just as the Supreme Court made a historic decision. A slave named Dred Scott had sued for his freedom because he had lived in free territory with his owner for many years. He felt he should no longer be a slave. The court ruled that enslaved people were property, not citizens, and remained slaves anywhere. Buchanan urged the nation to support what the court said. This made Northerners angry. And it split the nation more than ever.

Meanwhile, a small group of settlers in Kansas Territory had voted for a pro-slavery state constitution. Buchanan urged Congress to accept Kansas as a slave state. But when Congress asked for a new constitution representing *all voters* in the Kansas territory, settlers there strongly rejected slavery. Many felt Buchanan had tried to sneak Kansas in as a slave state over the wishes of people living there.

Buchanan was born in Pennsylvania. He had held public office and served President Jackson in Russia and Pierce in Britain as a diplomat. But as President, he wasn't able to bring the two sides of the nation together.

In the election of 1860, the antislavery candidate Abraham Lincoln was the winner. Between the election and Lincoln's taking office in 1861, seven southern states left the Union—South Carolina, Mississippi, Florida, Alabama, Georgia, Louisiana, and Texas. Buchanan left office with the nation on the edge of war. ✪

> ### Did You Know?
> When England's Prince of Wales came to visit the White House in 1860, so many guests came with him that Buchanan had to sleep in the hall.

◄ The U.S. broke apart over slavery during Buchanan's term.

KEY DATES

1858 First telegraph ► cable across the continent is completed, linking communication across the U.S.

1859 First oil well is drilled in Titusville, PA.

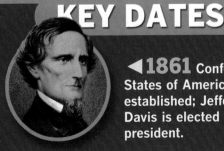

◄**1861** Confederate States of America is established; Jefferson Davis is elected president.

Abraham Lincoln

16th *President* ★ *1861-1865*

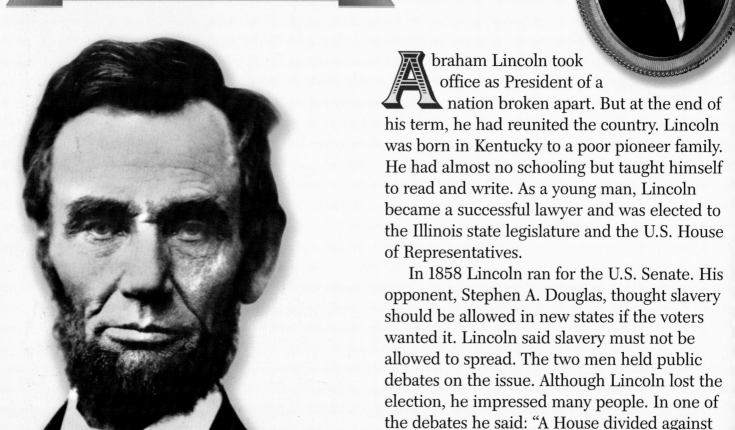

Abraham Lincoln took office as President of a nation broken apart. But at the end of his term, he had reunited the country. Lincoln was born in Kentucky to a poor pioneer family. He had almost no schooling but taught himself to read and write. As a young man, Lincoln became a successful lawyer and was elected to the Illinois state legislature and the U.S. House of Representatives.

In 1858 Lincoln ran for the U.S. Senate. His opponent, Stephen A. Douglas, thought slavery should be allowed in new states if the voters wanted it. Lincoln said slavery must not be allowed to spread. The two men held public debates on the issue. Although Lincoln lost the election, he impressed many people. In one of the debates he said: "A House divided against itself cannot stand." The "House" was the U.S., which was being divided by the issue of slavery.

When Lincoln was elected President in 1860, the "House" began to fall. By the time he took office in March 1861, seven states had left the U.S. and had formed the Confederate States of America. Within months Virginia, Arkansas,

◄ The President grew his famous beard after a young schoolgirl told him he would look better.

KEY DATES

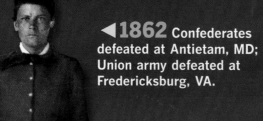

1861 Civil War breaks out when Confederate troops fire on Fort Sumter, SC.

◄**1862** Confederates defeated at Antietam, MD; Union army defeated at Fredericksburg, VA.

1863 Lincoln ► delivers Emancipation Proclamation, freeing all slaves in areas of conflict.

► In July 1863 nearly 90,000 Union soldiers fought 75,000 Confederate troops near Gettysburg, Pennsylvania.

North Carolina, and Tennessee would join them. Lincoln said he would fight to save the Union.

The fight began when rebels fired on Fort Sumter, a U.S. military base in South Carolina, on April 12, 1861, only six weeks after Lincoln's inauguration. The Civil War would last four years and take the lives of more than 600,000 Americans.

Lincoln thought slavery was wrong, but he thought it was legally protected in states where it already existed. When he became President, he promised not to interfere with states that had slaves. But when states began leaving the Union, Lincoln was determined to solve the issue of slavery. In early 1863 he issued the Emancipation Proclamation, which said all enslaved people living in Confederate states were free. More than 200,000 of these freedmen went north to fight in the war.

On April 9, 1865, Robert E. Lee, the Confederate general, surrendered at Appomattox Court House, Virginia, to U.S. General Ulysses S. Grant. The war was over and the Union had won.

◄ Lincoln visited troops at Antietam, Maryland, in October 1862 after the first major Union victory.

▲ First Lady Mary Todd Lincoln

Lincoln had led the nation through its most dangerous crisis. He saved the Union and put an end to slavery. He hoped to unite the nation, without anger or blame. Five days later, Lincoln and his wife, Mary, went to see a play. At the theater an actor named John Wilkes Booth shot the President. Lincoln died the next morning. ✪

Did You Know?

More Americans died in the Civil War than in all other U.S. wars put together.

1863 Union wins battle in Gettysburg, PA; Grant's Union troops win at Vicksburg, MS.

1864 Grant is made commander of all Union forces; Confederates abandon Atlanta.

◄ **1865** Union captures Richmond, VA; General Lee surrenders to Grant at Appomattox, VA.

Andrew Johnson

17th *President* ★ 1865-1869

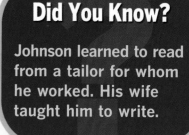

▲ Congressman Thaddeus Stevens of Vermont led the debate in Congress during Johnson's impeachment in 1868.

Did You Know?

Johnson learned to read from a tailor for whom he worked. His wife taught him to write.

Andrew Johnson was from a poor North Carolina family. He grew up believing that states should have the right to control slavery. But he also believed keeping the Union together was important. When Tennessee left the Union, Johnson, who was one of that state's senators, stayed in Congress. Even though he was a Democrat, Johnson was chosen to be Abraham Lincoln's running mate because of his loyalty to a united nation.

On April 15, 1865, Lincoln died and Andrew Johnson became President. His job was to help the North and South work together again. But he began by letting southern states pick their own leaders and decide how to treat the newly freed African Americans.

This angered the northern Republicans in Congress. They wanted to keep former southern leaders from serving in government after the war. And they wanted to get rid of southern laws designed to keep the four million former slaves from getting basic rights and freedoms.

Johnson did not want former slaves to be citizens. Over his protests, Congress in 1866 passed the 14th Amendment giving citizenship to African Americans. It also set up military governments in the South to help with Reconstruction, or rebuilding, after the war.

Johnson and Congress agreed on very little. And in 1868 Congress impeached the President, or charged him with breaking laws and abusing his powers. Congress held a trial to remove Johnson from office, but he was found not guilty. Nevertheless, it was a time of crisis for a nation trying to rebuild.

After the trial Johnson ended his term. He was elected senator from Tennessee again in 1874 but died the following year. ✪

◀ 1864 campaign flag

KEY DATES

1865 13th Amendment to the Constitution prohibits slavery.

1867 The U.S. buys Alaska Territory from Russia.

1869 First black ▶ U.S. diplomat is appointed, Ebenezer Bassett to Haiti.

Ulysses S. Grant

18th *President* ★ *1869-1877*

Ulysses Simpson Grant didn't seem to be good at anything. Born in Ohio, he was raised in a tannery. As a teenager Grant went to school at West Point, the United States military academy. He eventually fought in the Mexican War. There he made a name for himself as a horseman and led troops in the battle of Mexico City.

After the war Grant had a fight with his commander and was asked to leave the army. He returned to his family in Missouri but failed at several businesses. Then the Civil War began.

▲ An 1868 campaign medal honors the war hero.

When Grant returned to the military in 1861, the Union wasn't doing well. But Grant's troops soon won the Union's first major battle. And in 1863 his troops captured Vicksburg and ended the Confederacy's control of the Mississippi River. Lincoln was impressed with Grant's skills and eventually put him in charge of all the Union armies. On April 9, 1865, General Grant accepted the surrender of Confederate General Robert E. Lee at Appomattox Court House, Virginia.

Grant was a hero. He won the presidential election in 1868 and again in 1872, but Grant wasn't a strong political leader. During his terms, there were a lot of dishonest deals made by people in his government. Grant wasn't involved in the deals, but he did nothing to stop them. Because of the scandals, the Republican Party didn't select him to run for a third term.

In later years the publisher and author Mark Twain talked Grant into writing a book about his life and the war. He finished the book only days before he died. ✪

▼ Grant accepted Lee's surrender to end the Civil War.

Did You Know?

While President, Grant was stopped for speeding in his horse-drawn carriage. He had to walk back to the White House.

KEY DATES

1869 ▶
First railroad completed across continental U.S.

1872
Yellowstone becomes the world's first national park.

◀ 1876 Sitting Bull's Sioux Indians defeat Lt. Col. Custer's troops in Montana.

27

Rutherford B. Hayes

19th *President* ★ *1877-1881*

The presidency of Rutherford Birchard Hayes got off to a bumpy start. Hayes was accused of stealing the election of 1876 from his opponent, Samuel Tilden. Tilden had won the election, but the votes of three states were in dispute. A U.S. government committee was formed to rule on the problem. To get the southern states to accept him as President, Hayes agreed to remove federal troops from the South and let Southerners return to governing themselves. The deal pleased the committee and they awarded Hayes the electoral college votes. He was President—and got the not-so-nice nickname Ruther*fraud*!

Hayes was born in Ohio. As a young man, he practiced law until the start of the Civil War, when he volunteered to fight for the Union. While on the battlefield, Hayes was elected U.S. congressman from Ohio. Later he served two terms as governor before he was asked to run for President.

Hayes was an honest, decent man. He felt his job as President was "to wipe out the color line." But when he removed the last federal troops left in the South, ending Reconstruction, the laws giving equal rights to former slaves and whites were soon broken.

Hayes wanted to bring back the citizens' trust in government that was lost during the term of President Grant. He worked to change the spoils system, which was the way people got government jobs. He didn't run for a second term, but Hayes spoke out for equal education for African American children in the South. And he worked to end the death penalty for criminals.★

▲ Rutherford B. Hayes and his wife, Lucy

Did You Know?

Hayes was the first President to have a telephone and a typewriter in the White House.

KEY DATES

1877 Reconstruction ends; federal troops leave the South. Tchaikovsky writes *Swan Lake*.

◄**1879** Thomas Edison invents the electric light.

1881 Chicago ► White Stockings win National League pennant. William Herschel discovers the planet Uranus.

James Garfield

James A. Garfield never knew his father, who died while Garfield was an infant. Born and raised in Ohio, he helped his mother on the farm and seldom went to school. But when he was older, he studied religion, went to college, and became a professor. Garfield was elected an Ohio state senator and then fought in the Civil War. In 1862 he led a battle in Kentucky that gave the Union control of half the state. Soon he became the youngest major general in the military.

After the war Garfield served in the U.S. House of Representatives. As a congressman, he was one of the people on the committee who helped decide the 1876 presidential election. And he became the leader of the Republicans in Congress. In 1880 Garfield ran for President and won the election.

As President, Garfield wanted to make the U.S. economy stronger. And like Hayes, Garfield wanted to put an end to the spoils system, which gave members of the winning political party government jobs even if they weren't qualified.

Then tragedy struck. Charles J. Guiteau was angry because he wanted one of those jobs. Guiteau shot President Garfield at a Washington railroad station on July 2, 1881. Garfield lived for several weeks. Then a young inventor named Alexander Graham Bell was asked to try to locate the bullet with his new magnetic device. But all efforts to save the President failed and Garfield died on September 19, just six months after taking office.✪

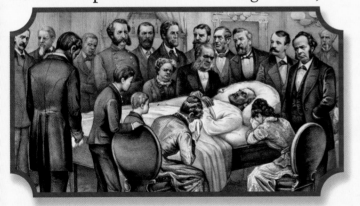

This campaign ▲ medal praised James Garfield as a "Soldier, Statesman, President."

Did You Know?
Garfield's mother, who raised him alone, was the first mother of a President to attend an inauguration.

▲ President Garfield on his deathbed in August 1881

KEY DATES

1881 ▶
The infamous frontier outlaw Billy the Kid dies in New Mexico.

1881 Booker T. Washington opens the Tuskegee Institute for African Americans.

1881 Clara Barton ▶ establishes the American Red Cross.

Chester A. Arthur

21st *President* ★ 1881–1885

▲ The press nicknamed the well-dressed President Elegant Arthur.

Chester Alan Arthur was the son of a minister who moved from town to town in Vermont and New York. As a young man, Arthur taught school to pay his way through college. During the Civil War, he was in charge of supplies and food for Union soldiers from New York. As a lawyer after the war, he worked on cases that helped African Americans get fair treatment. His work on these cases made Arthur popular with some politicians.

Before he was President, Arthur was in favor of the spoils system. Under President Grant he got a powerful job running the ports in New York because he had been helpful to the Republican Party.

▶ Shocked Americans rallied behind the new President in 1881.

Arthur then gave thousands of government jobs to other party members.

Because he could help deliver New York's important electoral votes, Arthur was picked as vice president on James Garfield's ticket. When the new President Garfield was killed, Arthur suddenly became President.

As President, Arthur did something no one expected. He worked to do away with the spoils system. He supported a system that gave out government jobs based solely on a person's abilities. And he continued work that President Garfield had started by going after people who used postal routes in the West to make money illegally.

Arthur had only one term as President. He didn't work hard to seek the nomination for election. What most people didn't know was that he was very sick. He died of kidney failure two years after the election of 1884. He is remembered as a President who was very honest and hardworking when no one expected him to be. ✪

Did You Know?

Known for elegant clothes and parties, Arthur thought the White House was shabby. He was the first to renovate it.

KEY DATES

1882 In an attempt to protect jobs, a ten-year ban starts on Chinese workers coming to the U.S.

1884 Population of the U.S. reaches fifty million.

1885 Arthur ▶ dedicates the Washington Monument on the first President's birthday.

Grover Cleveland

Did You Know?

Cleveland was supposed to serve in the Civil War but paid someone to fight in his place.

Grover Cleveland was the only President to serve two terms that were separated by another President's term. He was the 22nd and the 24th President.

Cleveland was born in New Jersey. His father died when he was sixteen and he had to give up his hope of going to college. Instead Cleveland worked for his uncle and got a job in a lawyer's office, where he learned the law.

Later Cleveland became the mayor of Buffalo, New York, and then governor of the state. He won the bitter election for President in 1884. Even though his opponent accused him of scandals in his private life, voters thought Cleveland was honest in his public life.

When Cleveland took office, there hadn't been a Democrat in the White House for twenty-four years. Cleveland felt there shouldn't be high taxes, or tariffs, on goods brought in from other countries. He wanted to increase foreign trade. He tried to reform the tariff laws, but he failed. Congress wanted to protect goods made in the U.S.

Cleveland lost the election of 1888 to Benjamin Harrison. Then he beat Harrison in 1892. When he started his second term, the economy was in bad shape and got worse. In the Great Panic of 1893, businesses failed and many Americans lost their jobs. When railroad workers went on strike near Chicago, Cleveland sent federal troops to restore order.

His actions against the workers and the long economic depression lost Cleveland the support of the country. At the end of his second term, he retired to Princeton, New Jersey. ✪

▼ In 1886 Cleveland married Frances Folsom in the first wedding ever held in the White House.

▲ Nicknamed Ugly Honest, Cleveland had no love for the press.

KEY DATES

1886 ▶
Statue of Liberty is dedicated in New York Harbor.

1893 New Zealand becomes first country in the world to give women the right to vote.

1894 Edison ▶ Corporation opens first motion-picture studio; films can be seen for 25 cents.

Benjamin Harrison

23rd *President* ★ 1889-1893

Benjamin Harrison came from a political family. His father was a U.S. congressman. His grandfather was William Henry Harrison, the ninth President of the U.S. And his great-grandfather had been a signer of the Declaration of Independence. So it wasn't surprising that Benjamin Harrison ended up in the White House.

Harrison was born in Ohio. He was a good student, went to college, and studied law. He then opened a law practice in Indiana. He served in the Civil War and became a U.S. senator from Indiana.

◄ **1888 election pin**

Harrison ran against President Grover Cleveland in the election of 1888. Cleveland wanted to lower the tax on imported goods. Harrison wanted a high tariff, which would raise the price on goods made in other countries and help U.S. businesses.

Harrison won. During his term, the tariffs were raised. But Harrison and Congress also worked to pass the Sherman Antitrust Act. This law was passed to protect people from high prices that a big U.S. company could

Did You Know?

First Lady Caroline Lavinia Harrison was responsible for bringing electricity to the White House.

charge consumers if it didn't have other companies competing with it for customers.

Harrison helped the United States gain respect in its dealings with other nations. He made sure foreign nations took U.S. goods in return for sending their goods to America. He stood firm against Chile when U.S. sailors were attacked there. And he led the very first Pan-American Conference, a meeting of the leaders of North, Central, and South America.

President Harrison had gotten a generous pension plan for Civil War veterans and their families. But Americans had grown tired of government spending and higher prices on imported goods. Former President Cleveland ran against Harrison again in 1892. This time Cleveland won. ✪

▼ Brigadier General Harrison, left, with other Union generals in 1865. As President twenty-five years later, he fought for retirement benefits for Civil War veterans.

KEY DATES

1889 Indian Territory is opened to white settlers. Eiffel Tower is built for Paris. ▶

1890 Last major battle of Indian Wars is at Wounded Knee in South Dakota.

1892 Ellis ▶ Island becomes main entry for foreigners coming to U.S.

William McKinley

During the Civil War, Rutherford Hayes wrote about one likable soldier under his command. "… every one admires [Captain McKinley] … as one of the bravest and finest young officers in the army."

The future 19th President was writing about the future 25th President. All his life William McKinley impressed people because he was so cheerful, wise, and respectful. McKinley was born in Ohio. He was a good student and worked as a teacher before the Civil War. After the war he studied law and went into politics. He was a U.S. congressman and then governor of Ohio.

In 1896 he ran as the Republican Party's candidate for President and won.

When McKinley took office, Cuba was at war for independence from Spain. Even though many Americans supported the Cubans, McKinley was eager to avoid war. But when the U.S. battleship *Maine* blew up in the harbor of Havana, Cuba, the Spanish were blamed. So the U.S. declared war on Spain. The Spanish-American War lasted only one hundred days. Cuba became free of Spanish rule. And the U.S. got the territories of Puerto Rico, Guam, and the Philippine Islands. The war helped make the U.S. a world power.

McKinley won reelection in 1900 by a wide majority. The next year he was at a fair in Buffalo, New York. Leon Czolgosz, an anarchist, or someone who thought that all government was bad, shot the President. Soldiers who had been guarding McKinley grabbed Czolgosz and began to beat him. As the wounded President was carried away, he told the soldiers not to hurt Czolgosz. McKinley died eight days later. ✪

▼ Campaign images, McKinley and Roosevelt here, appeared on everyday items.

Did You Know?

When McKinley was shot, he was taken to the hospital in an ambulance, making him the first President to ride in an automobile.

▼ "Remember the *Maine*" was the battle cry when the U.S. went to war with Spain.

KEY DATES

1897 First subway, or underground train, in the U.S. opens in Boston, MA.

1898 U.S. troops go to China to help protect Europeans from a rebellion against foreigners.

1900 Galveston, Texas, flooded by hurricane; 6,000 to 8,000 people die. U.S. population is more than seventy-five million.

Theodore Roosevelt

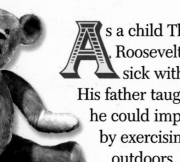

Did You Know?

The teddy bear was named for Roosevelt after it became known he refused to shoot a bear on a hunting trip.

As a child Theodore Roosevelt was often sick with asthma. His father taught him that he could improve himself by exercising and being outdoors. That lesson stuck with Roosevelt all his life.

After graduating from Harvard, Roosevelt married, entered politics, and was elected to the New York legislature. In 1884 his wife Alice died and a grieving Roosevelt moved to North Dakota, where he became a cowboy. Two years later he returned to New York and remarried. He served as head of New York City's police and then as assistant secretary of the Navy.

In 1898 the Spanish-American War began. Roosevelt formed a volunteer army called the Rough Riders and took them to Cuba. He became a war hero. On his return he was easily elected governor of New York. In 1900 he was elected William McKinley's vice president. Roosevelt became President when McKinley was killed. Voters liked him, and in the 1904 election Roosevelt was voted into office for four more years.

Roosevelt used his power as President to force businesses to follow rules of fairness in dealing with workers. But he broke up strikes that hurt the nation's economy. He set aside wilderness lands to keep them beautiful forever. He began the building of the Panama Canal to shorten the route for ships sailing east and west. After leaving office, Roosevelt went to Africa to hunt wild animals and went exploring in South America. He wrote more than forty books and ran for President again in 1912 as a third-party candidate. After an adventurous life, Roosevelt died peacefully in his sleep in 1919. ✪

◄ The future President led his Rough Riders to a major victory at the Battle of San Juan Hill in Cuba in the war against Spain in 1898.

KEY DATES

1903 Brothers Orville and Wilbur Wright make the first flight in a powered plane. ▶

1908 Ford Motor Co. produces the Model T.

1909 Explorers Robert E. Peary and Matthew Henson reach the North Pole. ▶

William H. Taft

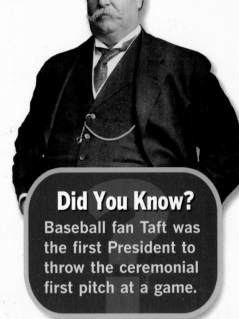

William Howard Taft was an unlikely presidential candidate. He was not good at saying things that would please voters. In fact, he disliked running for office. He once said, "Politics, when I am in it, makes me sick."

▲ Campaign pins from the 1908 election

Taft was born in Ohio. He went to Yale University and studied law in Cincinnati. His law practice led him to become a judge. His dream was to be a justice on the U.S. Supreme Court. Taft's wife, Nellie, however, had a bigger dream. She wanted to be First Lady.

Theodore Roosevelt and Taft were good friends and they admired each other's talents. When President McKinley sent Taft to the Philippines to help organize a new national government there, Roosevelt thought Taft did an excellent job. When Roosevelt was President, he made Taft his secretary of war. And when Roosevelt decided not to run again in 1908, he asked his supporters to choose Taft. Nellie had to convince Taft to accept the nomination.

Even though Taft said the campaign was "one of the most uncomfortable four months of my life," he won. As the new President, Taft disappointed Roosevelt. When Taft worked to break up large businesses like US Steel, Roosevelt felt Taft was being unfair. Roosevelt decided to run against Taft in the election of 1912. It split the Republican vote, and both men lost to the Democratic candidate.

After he left office, Taft taught law. Then in 1921 his longtime dream came true. He was named chief justice of the Supreme Court by President Harding. He said of those happy years, "I don't remember that I ever was President." ✪

◄Called the "crown prince" by the press, Taft might not have been elected without Teddy Roosevelt's support in 1908.

Did You Know?

Baseball fan Taft was the first President to throw the ceremonial first pitch at a game.

KEY DATES

1910 Boy Scouts of America is established.

1912 The ► *Titanic* sinks on its first voyage; more than 1,500 drown.

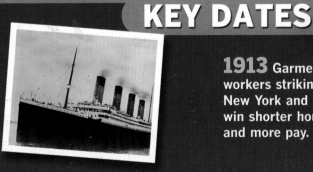

1913 Garment workers striking in New York and Boston win shorter hours and more pay.

Woodrow Wilson

28th *President* ★ *1913-1921*

Thomas Woodrow Wilson was born in Virginia in 1856 and grew up in Virginia and Georgia. His early memories were of a land torn by the Civil War.

As a young man, Wilson practiced law and then became a professor. He served as president of Princeton University and in 1910 was elected governor of New Jersey. Two years later he ran for U.S. President and won the election.

Wilson worked well with Congress. He helped bring about shorter workdays, made it possible for farmers to get loans, and kept children from working dangerous jobs.

When World War I began in Europe, Wilson hoped to keep the U.S. out of the war. But the war got worse. And in 1917 American spies discovered a plan for Mexico to join with Germany in fighting the U.S. If they won, the Germans had promised to give land from Texas to California back to Mexico. A year after the U.S. entered the war, Germany called for an end to the conflict.

Planning for the war's end, Wilson tried to ensure that the terms of peace would be fair. He had a plan, called Fourteen Points, to end secret agreements between nations, to open trade among all countries, and to free all occupied nations. He fought for the creation of the League of Nations, an organization of countries that would find peaceful solutions to conflicts. The League would eventually give way to the formation of the United Nations.

In 1919 Wilson toured the country to build support for the League. While on the tour, Wilson's health gave out and he suffered a stroke. Until the end of his second term in 1921, the President was seldom seen in public again. ✪

▼ **U.S. troops helped bring an end to World War I.**

Did You Know?

Wilson won the Nobel Peace Prize in 1919 for his efforts to secure lasting peace at the end of WWI.

Help us to win the vote

KEY DATES

1913 Panama Canal is completed. Zippers become widely used in clothing.

1917 U.S. ▶ declares war on Germany; enters World War I.

1920 19th Amendment ▶ to the Constitution gives women the right to vote. Babe Ruth is sold by the Boston Red Sox to the New York Yankees.

Warren G. Harding

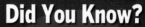

▲ The First Lady stood by her husband when he was hounded by gossip.

Warren Gamaliel Harding was born in Ohio in 1865. He worked for a newspaper, tried teaching, and studied law for a short time. Then he bought a small newspaper, the *Marion Star*, and made it successful. He was a state senator and then a U.S. senator.

Harding was a likable man. He had few enemies because he almost never said anything definite about what he believed and he seldom cast a vote as a senator. When two sides of the Republican Party couldn't agree on a candidate for President in 1920, Senator Harding was selected as a surprising compromise!

Woodrow Wilson had taken an active role in making the world better. But Harding felt the job of President was one with few responsibilities. He thought Congress ought to make the decisions. He worked to make government support the rights of businesses rather than individuals. Unlike Wilson, he made a point of not using his power to help farmers and people without jobs. He thought everyone who worked hard could make it without help.

Did You Know?

Harding was the first President elected after women could vote. But only 49 percent of all people who could vote did so.

Several of the men who worked closely with Harding got involved in taking bribes. One of Harding's advisors took a bribe in return for allowing an oil company to drill on land that had been set aside for the U.S. Navy. The land was in Teapot Dome, Wyoming, and this event became known as the Teapot Dome Scandal.

Needing time away from Washington and the troubles of his advisors, Harding and his wife, Flossie, took a long trip West in 1923. During their trip, Harding became ill. He died suddenly with his wife by his side. Later Flossie destroyed many of Harding's personal papers and his letters, hoping to avoid even more gossip and scandal. ✪

▲ Campaign cap for Harding and his running mate, Calvin Coolidge

KEY DATES

1921 U.S. declares official end of war with Germany and Austria. U.S. population is 107 million.

1922 Louis Armstrong's ▶ trumpet playing takes Chicago by storm; jazz replaces ragtime as nation's music craze.

1923 German shepherd Rin Tin Tin becomes Hollywood's first dog star.

Calvin Coolidge

30th *President* ★ *1923-1929*

John Calvin Coolidge was born in Vermont. His stern father taught him to serve the public. He became a lawyer and a state senator in Massachusetts. Later Coolidge became governor of the state. Then he became Warren Harding's vice president. He and his wife were visiting the family home in Vermont when they learned of Harding's death in 1923. His father, a justice of the peace, swore Coolidge in as the new President.

Not long after Coolidge took office, news spread of the illegal deals of some of Harding's advisors. But Coolidge hadn't taken part in the deals. Voters were grateful that the new man in the White House was honest. Coolidge was popular, and in 1924 the voters chose him for another four years.

The 1920s were good years for some Americans. Many businesses made lots of money. The population was growing. African Americans found jobs in northern cities. Jazz and nightclubs were popular during the Roaring Twenties. Many wealthy Americans were investing their money in fast-growing companies.

But the 1920s brought hard times for some people. Farmers struggled and rural businesses were losing money. Coolidge thought government shouldn't get involved. He didn't support labor unions fighting for better working conditions in mines or factories. Coolidge felt it was important to support big businesses rather than workers.

Coolidge also lowered taxes for the very wealthy. This led to big gaps between the poor and the rich. Very few people ran major businesses that controlled more than half the nation's economy. And more Americans lived in poverty than ever before. When Coolidge chose not to run again in 1928, he never gave a reason. But Coolidge told his wife he thought the nation's economy was going to collapse. ✪

Did You Know?

Often called Silent Cal for saying so little, Coolidge actually held 520 press conferences and gave monthly radio speeches.

▼ The President with Osage Indian guests in 1925

▲ 1924 campaign thimble

KEY DATES

1925 Nellie ▶ Tayloe Ross of Wyoming becomes first woman elected governor.

1927 Charles Lindbergh ▶ makes first solo nonstop flight across the Atlantic. Babe Ruth sets season record with sixty home runs.

1928 Alexander Fleming discovers penicillin.

Herbert Hoover

31st *President* ★ 1929-1933

Herbert Clark Hoover was born in Iowa in 1874. Both his parents died when he was young and he was raised by his uncle in Oregon. An average-to-failing student, Hoover set his sights on college. At Stanford University he studied engineering and became an expert on mines. He traveled all over the world running mines. He made his fortune too.

When World War I began, Hoover helped organize efforts to let 120,000 Americans stranded in Europe return to the U.S. Both before and after the war, he worked to solve the problem of starving Europeans. Hoover ran agencies that gave food and clothing to millions of people. And when he was working in Harding's administration as secretary of commerce, he managed relief efforts after huge floods along the Mississippi River. Hoover became known as a man who cared deeply for others and worked to help them. When he ran for President, he won easily.

In his first year as President, the U.S. economy failed. Millions of people lost their jobs. Businesses and banks closed. The Great Depression was the worst economic crisis the country has ever seen. Hoover did not understand how severe the crisis was. The failed economy wasn't his fault, but as things got worse, people blamed Hoover's leadership. They wanted the government to do more. Hoover's attempts to turn things around failed.

By 1932, with the nation in deep trouble, people wanted a new approach to solving the crisis. Hoover lost the election. He wasn't through with public service, though. Years later both Presidents Truman and Eisenhower asked Hoover to come out of retirement to help with government affairs. ✪

▲ Hoover lived thirty-one years after leaving the White House and continued to serve the nation.

Did You Know?

Millions of out-of-work Americans lived in tents or other temporary shelters called Hoovervilles.

KEY DATES

1929 ▶ The stock market crashes, causing panic for millions of investors.

1930 The planet Pluto is discovered by astronomers and is named by an eleven-year-old girl.

1931 "The Star-Spangled Banner" officially becomes U.S. national anthem.

Franklin D. Roosevelt

32nd *President* ★ *1933-1945*

On a cold, gray January day in 1933, Senator Jennings Randolph of West Virginia watched with thousands of people as Franklin Delano Roosevelt took the oath of office as President. "I was scared to death," said Randolph. "Everybody I knew had lost faith in the system of government. And then Roosevelt started to speak."

Roosevelt was from a wealthy New York family. At first he had trouble deciding what he wanted to do with his life. But then he became involved in politics. This was something he loved. He felt it was a way to help people who were less fortunate than he was.

Roosevelt started as a New York state senator. When he was thirty-eight, he developed an illness that left him unable to walk. Doctors treated him for polio. Roosevelt wasn't sure he'd ever run for office again, but he kept working for the Democrats. In 1928 he became governor of New York.

Four years later he was elected President. At his inauguration he said,

▲ First Lady Eleanor Roosevelt influenced her husband to help people in need.

Did You Know?

FDR was the only President to be elected to more than two terms in office. In 1951 the 22nd Amendment to the Constitution set a limit of two terms.

KEY DATES

1934 Severe drought hits central and southern plains states; Dust Bowl destroys farms.

1936 African ▶ American runner Jesse Owens wins four gold medals at Olympics in Berlin. China declares war on Japan.

1938 Germany annexes Austria. Anti-Jewish laws are passed in Italy. Howard Hughes flies around the world in 3 days and 19 hours. ▶

▲ The Japanese conducted a surprise attack on a U.S. naval air station in Pearl Harbor, Hawaii, on December 7, 1941.

"The only thing we have to fear is fear itself." Roosevelt was speaking to a nation that was suffering from the Great Depression. Millions of people had lost their jobs and millions were homeless. Roosevelt wanted people to know that the bad times wouldn't last forever.

As President, Roosevelt set up government agencies that created jobs for the unemployed. He pushed for laws that would make sure people got fair pay. He set up Social Security and insurance for the unemployed. He raised taxes on the wealthy to pay for

◄ FDR's "fireside chat" radio broadcasts were popular family events.

these programs. He called his programs a New Deal, a way to help Americans work their way out of the Depression.

Many people thought Roosevelt went too far. They said the government shouldn't get involved in business practices. But the voters were grateful for Roosevelt's programs. They reelected him in 1936 and again in 1940 and 1944!

When World War II began in Europe, Roosevelt felt the U.S. should go to the aid of the British. But most Americans felt the U.S. should stay out of the war. Then in 1941 German U-boats attacked American ships. And when Japan attacked Pearl Harbor on December 7, 1941, Roosevelt became a wartime President.

For forty-two months, U.S. troops fought with allies from Britain and the Soviet Union in battles in Europe, Africa, and Asia. Roosevelt worked closely with Britain's leader, Winston Churchill, and the Soviet leader, Joseph Stalin, to bring the war to an end. But he did not live to see the peace. He died in April 1945, just three months into his fourth term in office. The war in Europe ended the next month and Japan surrendered in September. ✪

▼ FDR didn't like to be photographed in a wheelchair. He worried that people would think less of him.

1939 England and France declare war on Germany. The film *The Wizard of Oz* is released in U.S. ▶

1941 U.S. declares war on Germany, Italy, and Japan; joins Allies in World War II.

1944 Allied troops invade Normandy, France, in D-day battle to defeat the Nazis.

Harry S. Truman

33rd *President* ★ *1945-1953*

▲ Captain Truman in World War I

▲ Truman, age 15

As a boy Harry S. Truman had to wear glasses, something not common in the late 1800s. His mother pushed him to play piano. Other children teased him and young Truman often felt he didn't fit in.

Born and raised in Missouri, Truman's farming family had to struggle, and money problems kept him from going to college. Instead, he worked in several jobs before settling down to run the family farm. During World War I, his National Guard unit was sent to fight in Europe.

When he returned home, he opened a men's clothing store. Truman first entered politics as a county court judge. Then he became a U.S. senator. When Roosevelt ran for his fourth term as President, he asked the well-respected Senator Truman to join his ticket. Truman had been vice president for only eighty-two days when President Franklin Roosevelt died. Suddenly Truman was President. "I felt like the moon, the stars, and all the planets had fallen on me," he said.

World War II wasn't over yet. A few weeks after Truman took office, Germany was defeated, but Japan was still fighting on. Truman made a difficult decision.

◄ "The buck stops here" was Truman's famous slogan about taking responsibility for his actions.

Did You Know?

Truman didn't have a middle name, only the initial *S.* His parents used the initial to honor their fathers, who had names starting with *S.*

KEY DATES

1945 United Nations is established. Germany and Japan surrender and World War II ends.

◄ **1946** Robert E. Byrd begins his expedition to the South Pole.

1947 *The Diary of Anne Frank* is published. Jackie Robinson becomes first black player to join Major League Baseball. ▶

TIME
THE WEEKLY NEWSMAGAZINE

He ordered the use of the atomic bomb. The U.S. bombed two Japanese cities, killing or wounding thousands. In a week the Japanese surrendered. Truman felt that, by ending the war quickly, he was saving lives in the long run.

▲ Two young North Korean boys are questioned by a U.S. soldier in 1950.

As World War II was ending, new problems began. The Soviet Union wanted to expand its control of countries in Eastern Europe with a form of government called communism. The U.S. tried to stop them. It was the start of a long, angry relationship between the two countries. The period was called the cold war. In 1950 war broke out between North and South Korea, which had been divided at the end of World War II. It was thought the Soviet Union played a role in the start of the conflict, and Truman sent U.S. troops there. But the North Koreans were being helped by Chinese troops. By 1953 the war stopped. Korea remained divided.

In the U.S. Truman tried to continue the policies of President Roosevelt with his own Fair Deal. He wanted the government to make sure that everyone had a job. He got laws passed to end unfair treatment for African Americans at work and in the military. And he worked for the G.I. Bill to provide college education for returning soldiers.

When Truman left office in 1952, people were tired of the tough times. They were ready for a change. Yet years later Truman is admired for his leadership during those times. ✪

◄ Atomic bombs dropped on Nagasaki (above) and Hiroshima led to a quick surrender by Japan.

1949 Indonesia gains independence from the Netherlands; Vietnam from France.

1950 North Korean troops attack South Korea. Only 1.5 million TV sets are in use in the U.S. ▶

1951 The 22nd Amendment to the Constitution limits U.S. President to two terms in office.

Dwight D. Eisenhower

People liked Ike, as young Dwight David Eisenhower was called growing up. After he was born in Texas, Eisenhower's family moved to Kansas and settled on a farm. The third of seven sons, Ike knew early he wanted a career in the army. So he went to the U.S. Military Academy at West Point.

Eisenhower did well in the army and was promoted many times. During World War II, he was put in charge of all Allied troops in Europe. By the end of World War II, he was the highest-ranking soldier in the military. When he returned home in 1945, he was a hero.

Did You Know?

Eisenhower was the first President sworn in on national television and the first to appear on color television.

Eisenhower passed up the chance to run for President as a Democrat in 1948. But in 1952 he decided to run for President as a Republican. He won easily.

▶ Ike's popular slogan

I LIKE IKE

As President, Eisenhower helped bring an end to the war that the U.S. was fighting in Korea. He tried to ease tensions between the Soviet Union and the U.S. He had spent most of his life in the army, but his parents had taught him to seek peaceful solutions.

At home the U.S. economy was doing well. Americans generally felt good about their life. But many African Americans weren't sharing in the good times or being treated fairly. In 1954 the Supreme Court ruled that schools separated by race were illegal. Eisenhower didn't like the ruling, but in 1957 he sent federal troops to a high school in Little Rock, Arkansas, to protect African American children entering the school. He felt he had to uphold the law. Yet when he left office, over 90 percent of African American children still attended separate schools. ✪

▲ Eisenhower proved to be a strong and able leader as supreme Allied commander in World War II.

KEY DATES

7053

1955 Rosa Parks is arrested ▶ in Montgomery, AL, for refusing to give up her seat on a bus to a white man; marks start of the civil rights movement.

1956 Minimum wage for workers is raised to $1.00 per hour from 75 cents.

1959 Hawaii becomes 50th state. More than eighty-five million TV sets are in use in the U.S.

John F. Kennedy

John Fitzgerald Kennedy came from a large and politically active Massachusetts family. His father dreamed that one day one of his sons would be President. Kennedy showed interest in politics early. In college at the age of twenty, he wrote a popular book, *Why England Slept*, about Great Britain not being prepared for a second war with Germany.

When the U.S. entered World War II, Kennedy joined the navy. He helped save his men when a boat he was commanding was sunk. After the war Kennedy was elected a U.S. congressman and then a senator from Massachusetts. In 1960 Kennedy ran for President against Vice President Richard Nixon. Their debates were the first ever shown on television. Kennedy looked young and smart, while Nixon appeared old and unprepared. Kennedy won in a close election.

As President, Kennedy faced several dangerous situations that involved the Soviet Union. At one point Soviet missiles were set up in Cuba, only ninety miles from Florida. Kennedy said he would use force if the missiles weren't removed. Finally the Soviet Union backed down.

Kennedy fought for a civil rights law to give equal rights to African Americans. He created the Peace Corps to help people in poorer nations improve their lives. And he pushed the U.S. space program forward.

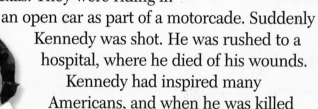

▲ 1960 campaign hat

On November 22, 1963, Kennedy and his wife, Jacqueline, were in Dallas, Texas. They were riding in an open car as part of a motorcade. Suddenly Kennedy was shot. He was rushed to a hospital, where he died of his wounds. Kennedy had inspired many Americans, and when he was killed the nation was deeply upset. The magical time Americans had called Camelot came to a sudden end. ✪

Did You Know?

At age 43, Kennedy was the youngest elected President. At 42, Teddy Roosevelt was the youngest to take office, after McKinley's death.

◀ The young President and First Lady made Americans hopeful.

KEY DATES

◀ **1961** Yuri Gagarin of Soviet Union is the first person to circle Earth in a spacecraft.

1962 First Lady gives tour of White House on TV; eight out of ten TVs are tuned in.

◀ **1963** Martin Luther King Jr. delivers "I Have a Dream" speech at March on Washington.

Lyndon B. Johnson

36th *President* ★ *1963-1969*

▲ 1964 campaign sticker

Fewer than two hours after John Kennedy was killed, Vice President Lyndon Baines Johnson became President. This powerful and persuasive man was ready for the job.

Johnson was born in Texas to a farming family. He went to college to be a teacher, then taught Hispanic students in a small Texas town. He wanted to make life better for people who struggled. So he went into politics. When World War II began, Johnson was a U.S. congressman, but he fought in the war. Years later he became the leader in the Senate.

Johnson was very good at working with people in Congress. He got them to pass laws to support his programs, called the Great Society. African Americans gained more rights with the

Did You Know?

President Johnson named the first African American to the Supreme Court: Thurgood Marshall.

Civil Rights Act and the Voting Rights Act. His War on Poverty started such programs as Head Start to provide early education for poor children. And he got Congress to pass Medicare and Medicaid plans to provide health care for the elderly and those least able to afford insurance.

Johnson won easily in the election of 1964. But a big problem was taking up his time in office. American troops had been in Vietnam for nearly ten years and the conflict was getting worse. Johnson sent many thousands more into the fight. But there were no signs the U.S. might win the war. Protests against the war in Vietnam grew. The country was divided over whether the U.S. should be fighting there at all.

Most polls indicated Johnson would have a difficult time being reelected. And Johnson no longer wanted to be the leader of a divided nation. At the end of his first full term, he retired to his ranch in Texas. ✪

▲ The President shakes the hands of soldiers on their way to fight in Vietnam in 1966.

KEY DATES

1964 Congress passes Civil Rights Act banning discrimination. The Beatles arrive in America and appear on TV. ▶

1967 First successful human heart transplant takes place.

1968 Martin Luther King Jr. is killed in Memphis, TN; presidential candidate Robert Kennedy is killed in Los Angeles, CA. ▶

Richard M. Nixon

▲ Nixon's resignation became effective at noon on August 9, 1974. He and First Lady Pat left the White House in the presidential helicopter that day.

Did You Know?

Nixon was the first President to visit all fifty states while in office.

Richard Milhous Nixon had a remarkable presidency. For many years China and the Soviet Union had been enemies of the U.S. Nixon visited both countries and set the stage for better relations with the two nations. Nixon also brought home the American soldiers who were fighting in Vietnam. And he was President when U.S. astronauts became the first humans to land on the moon.

But Nixon isn't remembered as a great President. In fact, he was the first and only U.S. President to have to resign. By the time he left office, many felt he had betrayed the trust of the American people.

Nixon was born in California in 1913. He became a lawyer and served in the navy during World War II. After the war he became a U.S. congressman and a senator. During the McCarthy Era in the 1950s when people were frightened of communism, Nixon led an investigation about spies in the U.S. government. No spies were found, but he made a name for himself. In 1953 he became Dwight Eisenhower's vice president.

Nixon lost the 1960 presidential election to John Kennedy but won the election eight years later. Then he easily won reelection. But in 1972 five men were arrested for breaking into the Democratic Party offices in a building called Watergate. The men worked for a committee set up to support Nixon's reelection. He and others lied to cover up the break-in. Congress accused Nixon of creating a secret police without its approval. Threatened with impeachment for his illegal activities, Nixon resigned in disgrace. ✪

▲ The President visits the *Apollo 11* crew in quarantine.

KEY DATES

1969 *Apollo 11* ▶ astronaut Neil Armstrong becomes the first human to walk on the moon.

1972 The compact disk, known as a CD, is invented.

1973 Vice President Spiro Agnew resigns office, accused of breaking laws while governor of Maryland.

Gerald R. Ford

38th *President* ★ *1974-1977*

The night Richard Nixon told the nation he was resigning his office, millions of Americans watched him on television. Among them was the vice president, who was at his home in Alexandria, Virginia, watching with his family. The next day Gerald Rudolph Ford and his wife, Betty, walked with the disgraced President and Mrs. Nixon to the helicopter waiting to take them away from the White House.

▲ The Fords walked with the Nixons as they left the White House.

Ford was born in Nebraska and was raised in Grand Rapids, Michigan. He was a good student and a star football player. He even played football at the University of Michigan. Ford went to Yale Law School before serving in the navy during World War II.

In 1948 Ford was elected a U.S. congressman from Michigan. He still held that office when President Nixon asked him to become vice president in 1973. Spiro Agnew, who had been vice president, had just resigned. When Ford became President a year later, he became the only person ever to hold the top U.S. office without having been chosen by the voters as either President or vice president.

As President, Ford gave former President Nixon a pardon, excusing him from any crimes he might have committed when he was President. Many people were unhappy about the pardon. They thought it would have been better to get everything out into the open, but Ford wanted to move on.

He had many other problems to deal with. The U.S. economy was in its worst decline since the Great Depression. And the cold war with the Soviet Union was heating up over nuclear missiles. Ford ran in the presidential election of 1976, hoping to win the office on his own. But he lost. Today Ford is often praised for ending the troubles from the Nixon years. ★

▶ Ford met with Soviet leader Leonid Brezhnev in Vladivostok in 1974.

Did You Know?

When he was born, Ford's name was Leslie Lynch King Jr. He was adopted and given his stepfather's name when he was two years old.

KEY DATES

1974 Henry "Hank" ▶ Aaron beats Babe Ruth's record of 714 home runs. Little League Baseball allows girls on teams.

1975 Over 6,000 life-sized pottery soldiers from 300 B.C. are discovered in China. The film *Jaws* is released in U.S. ▶

1976 U.S. celebrates its bicentennial, 200th birthday, with events across the country.

Jimmy Carter

39th *President* ★ *1977-1981*

Washington, D.C., hadn't seen a political outsider like Jimmy Carter in many years. He had no experience in Congress, was from the Deep South, was deeply religious, and appeared more at ease in denim jeans than a formal suit.

James Earl Carter Jr. always used the nickname Jimmy. He was born in Plains, Georgia, and raised on his family's peanut farm. He went to the United States Naval Academy at Annapolis, Maryland, where he studied nuclear physics. He served as a submarine commander before going back to the farm and entering politics. Carter was a state senator and then governor of Georgia before becoming President in 1976.

Carter was an honest man. He believed in making the government more efficient, ending unfair treatment of African Americans, and taking care of the environment.

But as President, Carter faced many problems. Energy use by Americans was high, and the oil-rich nations in the Middle East were raising the prices of oil and gas and cutting the supply. This led to a shortage of gasoline in the U.S. and long lines at the fuel pumps. Carter's Energy Bill helped reduce the shortages, but voters weren't happy about the problems.

In 1979 sixty-six Americans were taken hostage by religious extremists at the U.S. embassy in Iran. And in 1980 the U.S. failed in an effort to rescue the hostages. They weren't released until after Carter left office.

Carter wasn't reelected in 1980, but he did not slow down. He and his wife, Rosalynn, created a center for peace that helps nations settle differences. And in 2002 Carter won the Nobel Peace Prize for his efforts to find peaceful solutions to conflict and to promote human rights. ✪

◄ The former President builds houses for Habitat for Humanity. He and Rosalynn continue to work for the public good.

KEY DATES

1977 Carter forms Department of Energy in response to widespread energy crisis in U.S.

1978 Israel and Egypt sign a peace agreement at Camp David in the U.S.

Rollerblade

1980 U.S. athletes do not attend Olympics in Moscow to protest Soviet Union policies. ◄ Rollerblades are first introduced in U.S.

Ronald W. Reagan

40th *President* ★ *1981-1989*

Ronald Wilson Reagan was already well known to U.S. voters before he ever decided to run for office. He had been a movie and television actor for years.

Reagan was born in Illinois and lived over the store where his father worked. He loved sports and acting. After college Reagan got a job as a radio sports announcer. During World War II, he made training films for the army.

In 1966 Reagan was elected governor of California and held the office until 1975. Because of his acting background, Reagan was comfortable in front of a camera. Voters liked his relaxed, confident style and in 1980 elected him President.

Reagan's presidency began with exciting news from Iran. On the day Reagan took office, the Americans who had been held hostage for more than

▲ On air in Des Moines, Iowa

Did You Know?
Reagan was the only President to be wounded and survive an attempted assassination.

a year were freed. President Carter had worked out the release before leaving office. But the event set a positive tone for Reagan's first term.

Reagan thought that if the rich spent more money, it would "trickle down" and help all levels of the economy, so he lowered taxes for the wealthy. To keep the U.S. safe during the cold war, Reagan increased spending on weapons. Then in his second term, Reagan met with the leader of the Soviet Union, and their friendly talks led to a treaty in 1987 to reduce the supply of nuclear missiles.

When Reagan left office, many people felt he had made the world a safer place. He and the First Lady, Nancy, retired to California. Reagan died in 2004 after a long illness. ✪

▲ Soviet leader Mikhail Gorbachev and Reagan worked well together.

KEY DATES

1981 Astronauts John Young and Bob Crippen make first test flight of a space shuttle, *Columbia,* world's first reusable spacecraft.

1984 Soviet Union keeps its athletes out of the Summer Olympics in Los Angeles.

◀**1986** Space shuttle *Challenger* explodes after liftoff, killing all seven crew members. Tragedy is televised as it happens.

George H. W. Bush

41st President ★ 1989-1993

In an interview with TIME magazine one hundred days into his presidency, George Herbert Walker Bush said modestly, "I do hope that history will say we helped make things a little kinder and gentler."

Bush was born to a wealthy New England family. As a young man, he joined the navy during World War II and became its youngest pilot. After the war Bush married, went to college, and moved to Texas to enter the oil business.

Bush's father had been a U.S. senator from Connecticut, and Bush wanted to enter politics. While living in Texas, he was elected as a U.S. congressman. Eventually Bush served as the U.S. representative to the United Nations and China and as director of the Central Intelligence Agency, the nation's spy organization. Bush served as Ronald Reagan's vice president for two terms. In 1988 he was elected President on his own.

Bush was President for one term, but there were big changes during those years.

The long period of cold war between the U.S. and the Soviet Union came to an end during Bush's term.

As President, Bush sent U.S. soldiers to several trouble spots. The most important was Iraq. In the well-planned Operation Desert Storm, the U.S. and U.N. forces scored a victory in forcing Iraq's invading troops out of the oil-rich country of Kuwait.

Even though he had many successes in office, Bush didn't get reelected President in 1992. The U.S. economy wasn't strong. While running for office, he had promised, "Read my lips. No new taxes." But the weak economy caused him to raise taxes. Voters weren't happy with his handling of the economic problems. At the end of his term, Bush returned home to Texas and Maine. ✪

◀ Success in Kuwait gave Bush high approval ratings for a short period.

Did You Know?

Two of George Bush's sons were elected governors: George W. Bush of Texas in 1994 and Jeb Bush of Florida in 1998.

KEY DATES

1989 More than a million Chinese students rally for democracy in Beijing's Tiananmen Square; thousands killed in government crackdown.

1990 South Africa frees ▶ Nelson Mandela after 27 years in prison. East and West Germany reunited. World Wide Web launches.

1991 Lithuania, Estonia, and Latvia win independence from Soviet Union.

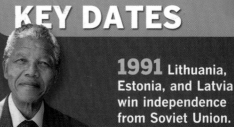

William J. Clinton

42nd *President* ★ *1993-2001*

Bill Clinton was a high school senior with thoughts of becoming a professional musician when he went to a youth conference in Washington, D.C. At a White House reception, Clinton got to shake hands with President John F. Kennedy. The future President Clinton often said that moment changed his life.

Bill Clinton was born William Jefferson Blythe III in Hope, Arkansas. His father was killed in an accident three months before his birth. His mother married a man named Roger Clinton, and years later Bill took the new family name.

Clinton was an excellent student. He went to college at Georgetown University and then to Oxford University in England. Returning home, he went to Yale Law School, where he met and married Hillary Rodham, a student from Illinois.

Eventually Clinton returned home to Arkansas, where he taught law. Soon he was elected attorney general and then governor of Arkansas. In

Did You Know?

While campaigning for President, Clinton played his saxophone on national television.

◄ Young Clinton was inspired by JFK.

KEY DATES

1994 Major League Baseball players go on strike; season ends in August. Nelson Mandela elected president of South Africa.

1995 U.S. terrorists bomb federal building in Oklahoma City, OK; 168 people killed. DVDs are first introduced.

◄ **1996** Madeleine Albright becomes first female U.S. secretary of state. The Taliban, who are Muslim fundamentalists, take over Afghanistan.

► Clinton struggled to build trust between Israel's Menachim Begin and Palestinian Authority's Yasser Arafat.

1992 he ran as the Democratic candidate against President Bush and won.

President Clinton wanted to improve the economy and stop the government from spending more than it took in. Clinton's budget plan increased taxes on the wealthy and provided tax cuts to high-tech companies to encourage their growth. His plan worked and created a surplus of money in the federal budget for the first time in thirty years. The President and First Lady also worked to improve health care in the U.S. The U.S. is the only modern nation in the world that doesn't provide health care for all its citizens. But the Clintons couldn't get Congress to agree to their complicated plan.

In other parts of the world, Clinton tried to move people toward peace in the Middle East. He encouraged more trade with China. And he sent U.S. troops to help in conflicts in Bosnia and the Serbian province of Kosovo. Clinton worked closely with Boris Yeltsen, the leader of Russia, to bring the fighting to an end.

Clinton was elected to a second term in 1996. During both his terms, he faced charges of illegal behavior but was never found guilty. In late 1999 he was impeached, which means that he was accused by the House of Representatives of breaking the law. In a trial in the U.S. Senate, Clinton was cleared of all charges.

Clinton left the White House still a very popular President. After retiring to New York, he wrote a best-selling book about his life. In 2004 Clinton joined former President George H. W. Bush in heading U.S. efforts to help the victims of a major tsunami. And he continues to remain active in Democratic politics. ✪

◄ The Clintons with Vice President Al Gore and his wife, Tipper

1998 ► European Union nations agree on a single currency called the euro. *Harry Potter and the Sorcerer's Stone* published in U.S.

1999 Michael ► Jordan retires from Chicago Bulls. U.S. women's soccer team defeats China to win World Cup.

2000 First Lady Hillary Clinton elected to U.S. Senate from New York. South Carolina removes Confederate flag from state capitol.

George W. Bush

Geeorge Walker Bush became President as a result of an unusual election. It was held on November 7, 2000, but the winner wasn't known until December 12. The election had been so close that many people wanted votes in Florida and other states recounted. Finally the U.S. Supreme Court ruled that it was time to stop recounting the votes. Bush, the Republican candidate, was declared the winner over Vice President Al Gore.

Bush came from a political family. His grandfather Prescott had been a senator from Connecticut. His father, George, had been the 41st President, and his brother Jeb was the governor of Florida.

Bush was born in Connecticut and grew up in Texas. He went to Yale and Harvard and then went into the oil business in Texas. He bought the

◀ The President and First Lady Laura Bush in 2001

Did You Know?

Bush named the first African Americans as secretaries of state: Colin Powell and Condoleezza Rice.

KEY DATES

2001 The worst terrorist attack ever on U.S. soil takes place on the morning of September 11.

2002 Fox reality TV show *American Idol* debuts. More than half the U.S. population now uses the Internet.

◀ **2003** At age thirteen, Keisha Castle-Hughes is youngest person nominated for best-actress Oscar for role in *Whale Rider*. Space shuttle *Columbia* explodes, killing all seven astronauts aboard.

Texas Rangers baseball team with several other business people. Then in 1994 he was elected governor of Texas. Six years later he became President of the U.S.

Bush got off to a successful start as President. He wanted to lower taxes. And because the government had a budget surplus from the Clinton years, Congress agreed. He also got a bill passed, called No Child Left Behind, that increased funds for education and put strict rules on states to raise test scores of children.

But the biggest challenge he would face happened on September 11, 2001. Terrorists hijacked airplanes that morning and flew two of them into the World Trade Center towers in New York City. Another plane was flown into the Pentagon in Washington, D.C., and a fourth was forced to crash in Pennsylvania. Almost 3,000 people died.

The U.S. had been attacked by a terrorist organization called Al Qaeda led by a man named Osama bin Laden. Less than a month after the attacks, Bush ordered U.S. troops to Afghanistan, where the country's leaders were thought to be hiding bin Laden. The U.S. was successful in changing the country's leadership, but bin Laden wasn't captured.

In 2003 Bush thought that Iraq might

▲ Bush visited rescue workers in New York and Washington and promised a "war on terrorism."

have weapons that could threaten the U.S. and other nations in the world. Against the wishes of many Americans and leaders around the world, Bush sent soldiers to invade Iraq. In six weeks they brought down the Iraqi government. Since that time, U.S. soldiers and advisors have been trying to get the country working again. And the troops are still fighting Iraqis who don't want the U.S. there.

Bush won reelection in 2004. But the President, who had promised to improve relations between Democrats and Republicans when he campaigned in 2000, leads a nation that is divided over his policies and the war in Iraq. ✪

▲ U.S. troops lead the efforts in rebuilding Iraq in 2005.

◀ **2004** Soccer star Freddy Adu, age thirteen, becomes youngest ever U.S. pro athlete; plays for D.C. United.

2004 A powerful earthquake near Indonesia causes a tsunami killing more than 170,000 people in Asia and East Africa.

◀ **2005** *Huygens* space probe lands on Titan; joint effort between NASA, European Space Agency, and Italy took seven years to reach Saturn's largest moon.

▲ Martha Washington

The Nation's First Ladies

▲ Dolley Madison

Martha Washington became the first wife of a U.S. President in 1789. She took on the job of being hostess to all those who came to visit the leader of the new nation. But Martha preferred the busy, quiet home life she left behind. She said she felt like a "state prisoner." But like her husband, she believed it was her duty to serve the public.

The early First Ladies had been strong supporters of the American Revolution and took personal risks along with their husbands. Abigail Adams was her husband John's most trusted friend and closest advisor.

▼ Abigail Adams

They wrote almost daily letters to each other during his many travels across the colonies and in Europe.

Dolley Madison acted as hostess for President Thomas Jefferson, whose wife had died. She continued in that job when her own husband, James, became President. Unlike Martha Washington, Dolley loved being a hostess and she became a social celebrity. During the War of 1812, Dolley rescued some important papers and a portrait of George Washington from the White House as the British troops invaded.

Although Dolley Madison was called America's First Lady at her funeral, it was Lucy Hayes, wife of Rutherford Hayes, who was first given the title by a reporter. It caught on, and wives of Presidents have been called First Lady ever since.

When Woodrow Wilson became ill in 1919, his second wife, Edith Wilson, became the link between the President and the public. In fact, some people felt that she was running the country for a time, but she didn't make decisions or create policy.

▲ Edith Wilson

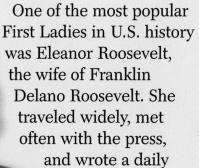

▶ Lady Bird Johnson

One of the most popular First Ladies in U.S. history was Eleanor Roosevelt, the wife of Franklin Delano Roosevelt. She traveled widely, met often with the press, and wrote a daily newspaper column. Eleanor was a big influence on her husband. And she was involved in the labor, civil rights, and women's movements as well as shaping New Deal policies. The press called her First Lady of the World.

Jacqueline Kennedy brought a new level of style and culture to the White House. She helped create the center for performing arts that was later named after her husband, John F. Kennedy. The public loved "Jackie," and many women imitated her fashion style. In 1962 she renovated the White House and gave the nation its first televised tour.

All the Presidents' wives of the past four decades have taken a stand on issues that they believed in. Jackie Kennedy urged government support for the arts. Lady Bird Johnson worked to beautify the nation's highways. Betty Ford supported the passage of the Equal Rights Amendment and brought the modern women's movement into the cultural mainstream. Rosalynn Carter became an expert on policy in Latin America and supported aid for the elderly. Barbara Bush worked to end illiteracy. Hillary Rodham Clinton was actively involved in policies shaping health care in the U.S. And she became the only First Lady who had her own political career when she was elected to the U.S. Senate from New York. The current First Lady, Laura Bush, is a strong supporter of libraries and reading programs for children.

All of the First Ladies had one thing in common: They were women. In the future the press may need to come up with a new term for the *husband* of the President! ✪

◀ Jackie Kennedy

▼ Laura Bush

Presidents at a Glance

Seven Presidents were born in Ohio, but what state is the home of more Presidents than any other? Who was the first President born west of the Mississippi River? Which President lived to be the oldest? How many Presidents died on the Fourth of July? Who was the only President born on the Fourth of July?

The data here will help you answer these questions and more about the forty-two men who have served as President of the United States. To learn more, go to timeforkids.com/HH and look for presidents in the resources listed.

Oh, and one more. Which President lost reelection in 1980 to a former movie star? ✪

George Washington

Born: Feb. 22, 1732, in Westmoreland Co., VA
Died: Dec. 14, 1799, at Mount Vernon, VA
Political Party: Federalist
Vice President: John Adams
Wife: Martha Dandridge Custis
Children: Stepchildren John, Martha

John Adams

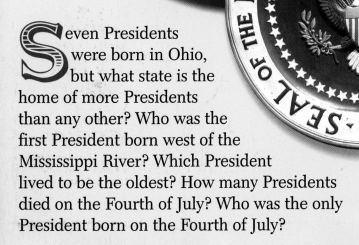

Born: Oct. 30, 1735, in Braintree (now Quincy), MA
Died: July 4, 1826, in Quincy, MA
Political Party: Federalist
Vice President: Thomas Jefferson
Wife: Abigail Smith
Children: Abigail, John Quincy, Susanna, Charles, Thomas Boylston

Thomas Jefferson

Born: April 13, 1743, in Albemarle Co., VA
Died: July 4, 1826, in Charlottesville, VA
Political Party: Democratic-Republican
Vice Presidents: Aaron Burr, George Clinton
Wife: Martha Skelton
Children: Martha, Mary, Lucy Elizabeth[3]

James Madison

Born: March 16, 1751, in Port Conway, VA
Died: June 28, 1836, in Montpelier, VA
Political Party: Democratic-Republican
Vice Presidents: George Clinton, Elbridge Gerry
Wife: Dolley Payne Todd
Children: None

James Monroe

Born: April 28, 1758, in Westmoreland Co., VA
Died: July 4, 1831, in New York City, NY
Political Party: Democratic-Republican
Vice President: Daniel D. Tompkins
Wife: Elizabeth Kortright
Children: Eliza, James Spence, Maria Hester[1]

John Quincy Adams

Born: July 11, 1767, in Quincy, MA
Died: Feb. 23, 1848, in Washington, DC
Political Party: Democratic-Republican
Vice President: John C. Calhoun
Wife: Louisa Catherine Johnson
Children: George Washington, John, Charles Francis, Louisa

1 One other child died in infancy. 2 Two other children died in infancy. 3 Three other children died in infancy.

Andrew Jackson

Born: March 15, 1767, in The Waxhaws, SC
Died: June 8, 1845, in Nashville, TN
Political Party: Democratic
Vice Presidents: John C. Calhoun, Martin Van Buren
Wife: Rachel Robards
Children: adopted nephew Andrew Jr.

Martin Van Buren

Born: Dec. 5, 1782, in Kinderhook, NY
Died: July 24, 1862, in Kinderhook, NY
Political Party: Democratic
Vice President: Richard M. Johnson
Wife: Hannah Hoes
Children: Abraham, John, Martin Jr., Smith[1]

William Henry Harrison

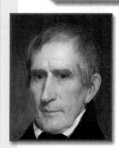

Born: Feb. 9, 1773, in Charles City Co., VA
Died: April 4, 1841, in Washington, DC
Political Party: Whig
Vice President: John Tyler
Wife: Anna Tuthill Symmes
Children: Elizabeth, John, Lucy, William, John Scott, Mary, Carter, Anna, James

John Tyler

Born: March 29, 1790, in Charles City Co., VA
Died: Jan. 18, 1862, in Richmond, VA
Political Party: Whig
Vice President: None
Wives: Letitia Christian, Julia Gardiner
Children: Mary, Robert, John Jr., Letitia, Elizabeth, Anne, Alice, Tazewell, David, John Alexander, Julia, Lachlan, Lyon, Robert Fitzwalter, Pearl[1]

James K. Polk

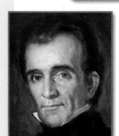

Born: Nov. 2, 1795, in Mecklenburg Co., NC
Died: June 15, 1849, in Nashville, TN
Political Party: Democratic
Vice President: George M. Dallas
Wife: Sarah Childress
Children: None

Zachary Taylor

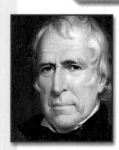

Born: Nov. 24, 1784, in Montebello, VA
Died: July 9, 1850, in Washington, DC
Political Party: Whig
Vice President: Millard Fillmore
Wife: Margaret Mackall Smith
Children: Ann, Sarah Knox, Octavia, Margaret, Mary Elizabeth, Richard

Millard Fillmore

Born: Jan. 7, 1800, in Summerhill, NY
Died: March 8, 1874, in Buffalo, NY
Political Party: Whig
Vice President: None
Wife: Abigail Powers
Children: Millard Powers, Mary Abigail

Franklin Pierce

Born: Nov. 23, 1804, in Hillsboro, NH
Died: Oct. 8, 1869, in Concord, NH
Political Party: Democratic
Vice President: William R. King
Wife: Jane Means Appleton
Children: Frank Robert, Benjamin[1]

James Buchanan

Born: April 23, 1791, in Cove Gap, PA
Died: June 1, 1868, in Lancaster, PA
Political Party: Democratic
Vice President: John C. Breckinridge
Wife: None
Children: None

Abraham Lincoln

Born: Feb. 12, 1809, in Hardin Co., KY
Died: April 15, 1865, in Washington, DC
Political Party: Republican
Vice Presidents: Hannibal Hamlin, Andrew Johnson
Wife: Mary Todd
Children: Robert Todd, Edward, William Wallace, Thomas (Tad)

Andrew Johnson

Born: Dec. 29, 1808, in Raleigh, NC
Died: July 31, 1875, in Carter Co., TN
Political Party: Democratic
Vice President: None
Wife: Eliza McCardle
Children: Martha, Charles, Mary, Robert, Andrew

Ulysses S. Grant

Born: April 27, 1822, in Point Pleasant, OH
Died: July 23, 1885, in Mt. McGregor, NY
Political Party: Republican
Vice Presidents: Schuyler Colfax, Henry Wilson
Wife: Julia Boggs Dent
Children: Frederick, Ulysses, Ellen, Jesse

Rutherford B. Hayes

Born: Oct. 4, 1822, in Delaware, OH
Died: Jan. 17, 1893, in Fremont, OH
Political Party: Republican
Vice President:
William A. Wheeler
Wife: Lucy Ware Webb
Children: Birchard Austin, James, Rutherford, Fanny, Scott Russell[3]

James Garfield

Born: Nov. 19, 1831, in Orange Township, OH
Died: Sept. 19, 1881, in Elberon, NJ
Political Party: Republican
Vice President:
Chester A. Arthur
Wife: Lucretia Rudolph
Children: Harry, James R., Mary, Irvin, Abram[2]

Chester A. Arthur

Born: Oct. 5, 1829, in North Fairfield, VT
Died: Nov. 18, 1886, in New York City, NY
Political Party: Republican
Vice President:
None
Wife: Ellen Herndon
Children: William, Chester Jr., Nellie

Grover Cleveland

Born: March 18, 1837, in Caldwell, NJ
Died: June 24, 1908, in Princeton, NJ
Political Party: Democratic
Vice Presidents:
Thomas Hendricks, Adlai Stevenson
Wife: Frances Folsom
Children: Ruth, Esther, Marion, Richard, Francis Grover

Benjamin Harrison

Born: Aug. 20, 1833, in North Bend, OH
Died: March 13, 1901, in Indianapolis, IN
Political Party: Republican
Vice President:
Levi P. Morton
Wife: Caroline Lavinia Scott
Children: Russel Benjamin, Mary

William McKinley

Born: Jan. 29, 1843, in Niles, OH
Died: Sept. 14, 1901, in Buffalo, NY
Political Party: Republican
Vice Presidents:
Garret Hobart, Theodore Roosevelt
Wife: Ida Saxton
Children: Katherine, Ida

Theodore Roosevelt

Born: Oct. 27, 1858, in New York City, NY
Died: Jan. 6, 1919, in Oyster Bay, NY
Political Party: Republican
Vice President:
Charles W. Fairbanks
Wives: Alice Lee, Edith Kermit Carow
Children: Alice, Theodore, Kermit, Ethel, Archibald, Quentin

William H. Taft

Born: Sept. 15, 1857, in Cincinnati, OH
Died: March 8, 1930, in Washington, DC
Political Party: Republican
Vice President:
James S. Sherman
Wife: Helen (Nellie) Herron
Children: Robert Alphonso, Helen, Charles Phelps

Woodrow Wilson

Born: Dec. 28, 1856, in Staunton, VA
Died: Feb. 3, 1924, in Washington, DC
Political Party: Democratic
Vice President:
Thomas R. Marshall
Wives: Ellen Louise Axson, Edith Bolling Galt
Children: Margaret, Jessie, Eleanor

Warren G. Harding

Born: Nov. 2, 1865, in Bloomington Grove, OH
Died: Aug. 2, 1923, in San Francisco, CA
Political Party: Republican
Vice President:
Calvin Coolidge
Wife: Florence Kling
Children: None

Calvin Coolidge

Born: July 4, 1872, in Plymouth Notch, VT
Died: Jan. 5, 1933, in Northampton, MA
Political Party: Republican
Vice President:
Charles G. Dawes
Wife: Grace Anna Goodhue
Children: John, Calvin Jr.

Herbert Hoover

Born: Aug. 10, 1874, in West Branch, IA
Died: Oct. 20, 1964, in New York City, NY
Political Party: Republican
Vice President:
Charles Curtis
Wife: Lou Henry
Children: Herbert Jr., Allan

Franklin D. Roosevelt

Born: Jan. 30, 1882, in Hyde Park, NY
Died: April 12, 1945, in Warm Springs, GA
Political Party: Democratic
Vice Presidents: John Garner, Henry Wallace, Harry S. Truman
Wife: Anna Eleanor Roosevelt
Children: Anna Eleanor, James, Elliott, Franklin Delano Jr., John[1]

Harry S. Truman

Born: May 8, 1884, in Lamar, MO
Died: Dec. 26, 1972, in Kansas City, MO
Political Party: Democratic
Vice President: Alben W. Barkley
Wife: Elizabeth (Bess) Virginia Wallace
Children: Margaret

Dwight D. Eisenhower

Born: Oct. 14, 1890, in Denison, TX
Died: March 28, 1969, in Washington, DC
Political Party: Republican
Vice President: Richard M. Nixon
Wife: Marie (Mamie) Geneva Doud
Children: Doud Dwight, John Sheldon

John F. Kennedy

Born: May 29, 1917, in Brookline, MA
Died: Nov. 22, 1963, in Dallas, TX
Political Party: Democratic
Vice President: Lyndon B. Johnson
Wife: Jacqueline Lee Bouvier
Children: Caroline, John[1]

Lyndon B. Johnson

Born: Aug. 27, 1908, near Stonewall, TX
Died: Jan. 22, 1973, in San Antonio, TX
Political Party: Democratic
Vice President: Hubert H. Humphrey
Wife: Claudia Alta (Lady Bird) Taylor
Children: Lynda Bird, Luci Baines

Richard M. Nixon

Born: Jan. 9, 1913, in Yorba Linda, CA
Died: April 22, 1994, in New York City, NY
Political Party: Republican
Vice Presidents: Spiro T. Agnew, Gerald R. Ford
Wife: Thelma Catherine (Pat) Ryan
Children: Patricia, Julie

Gerald R. Ford

Born: July 14, 1913, in Omaha, NE
Political Party: Republican
Vice President: Nelson A. Rockefeller
Wife: Elizabeth (Betty) Anne Bloomer
Children: Michael, John, Steven, Susan

Jimmy Carter

Born: Oct. 1, 1924, in Plains, GA
Political Party: Democratic
Vice President: Walter F. Mondale
Wife: Eleanor Rosalynn Smith
Children: John William, James Earl III, Jeffrey, Amy Lynn

Ronald W. Reagan

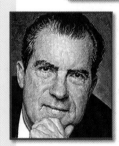

Born: Feb. 6, 1911, in Tampico, IL
Died: June 5, 2004, in Bel-Air, CA
Political Party: Republican
Vice President: George H. W. Bush
Wives: Jane Wyman, Nancy Davis
Children: Maureen, Michael, Patti, Ronald Jr.[1]

George H.W. Bush

Born: June 12, 1924, in Milton, MA
Political Party: Republican
Vice President: J. Danforth (Dan) Quayle
Wife: Barbara Pierce
Children: George Walker, Robin, John Ellis, Neil, Marvin, Dorothy

William J. Clinton

Born: Aug. 19, 1946, in Hope, AR
Political Party: Democratic
Vice President: Albert Gore Jr.
Wife: Hillary Rodham
Children: Chelsea

George W. Bush

Born: July 6, 1946, in New Haven, CT
Political Party: Republican
Vice President: Richard Cheney
Wife: Laura Welch
Children: Barbara, Jenna

1 One other child died in infancy. 2 Two other children died in infancy. 3 Three other children died in infancy.

Welcome to the WHITE HOUSE

When a new President is elected, it's time to pack up and move into the grand mansion at 1600 Pennsylvania Avenue in Washington, D.C. This White House has been home to every presidential family except George Washington's. In its rooms our leaders have planned wars, signed important laws and treaties, welcomed foreign leaders, and made historic speeches.

In 1790 Washington asked Congress to determine where the President's house should be built. The nation's capital at the time was Philadelphia. But Congress had set aside a large, empty section of land in which to build a new capital city. And it was here, in a city eventually named for the first President, that architect James Hoban began construction in 1792 of the President's house. In 1800 President John Adams and his family moved into the cold, damp, and unfinished mansion. Since then it has survived two fires and numerous remodelings.

The home and office of the U.S. President is the only private residence of a head of state that is free and open to the public. Each year hundreds of thousands of visitors tour the White House. Here's your chance to take a look for yourself. ★

Private Living Quarters

State Dining Room

West Wing

Second Floor

Blue Room

Red Room

Green Room

East Room

First Floor

Map Room

Diplomatic Reception Room

Library

China Room

East Wing

Vermeil Room

Ground Floor

Postcards from Washington, D.C.

A Capital Place to Visit!

Each year some twenty million people go to Washington, D.C., to see its historic monuments and museums. Here are some sights that tourists can visit. ★

Jefferson Memorial

In 1934 Congress approved the construction of a memorial to honor Thomas Jefferson. The memorial, like Jefferson's home, Monticello, in Virginia, is based on the Pantheon—a building in Rome, Italy. The circular marble structure was finished in 1943. If you visit in early spring, you'll get to see the monument surrounded by blossoming cherry trees.

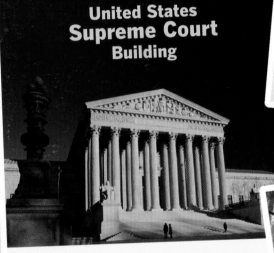

United States Supreme Court Building

The style of this classical building fits right in with other government structures in the neighborhood. Built in the 1930s, the building is home to our nation's top judges. Two bronze doors weigh thirteen thousand pounds each and neatly slide into wall recesses. The entire building is made of marble from Georgia and Vermont.

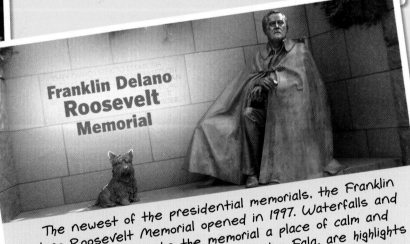

Franklin Delano Roosevelt Memorial

The newest of the presidential memorials, the Franklin Delano Roosevelt Memorial opened in 1997. Waterfalls and large shade trees make the memorial a place of calm and quiet. Statues of Roosevelt and his dog, Fala, are highlights of the structure, as are some of the President's famous words carved into the granite walls. There is also an exhibit about Eleanor Roosevelt, the President's wife.

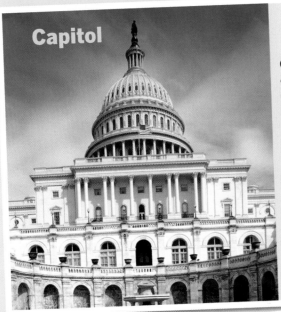

Capitol

This is where Congress meets and conducts business. Construction of the building started in 1793 and was finished in 1865. The Capitol's most recognizable feature is the 180-foot-high cast iron dome of the Great Rotunda. The dome weighs nine million pounds.

Lincoln Memorial

Architect Henry Bacon modeled the marble, granite, and limestone building after the Greek Parthenon. Completed in 1922, the Lincoln Memorial has thirty-six columns, which represent the number of states in the Union at the time of Lincoln's death in 1865. Inside you'll see a statue of President Lincoln and read his famous Gettysburg Address.

Washington Monument

It took nearly a century to plan and build this very tall monument to George Washington, which was opened to visitors in 1888. The narrowing shaft, or obelisk, is made of stone and covered in marble. It stands just over 555 feet high—as tall as a fifty-story building. If you climb the 896 steps to the top, you'll get a postcard view of the city below.

Did You Know?

Residents and visitors to Washington can thank African American Benjamin Banneker (1731—1806) for helping create the capital city. In 1791 President Washington hired Banneker and two others to survey the land on which the city would be built. Then the head planner, Pierre L'Enfant, got fired from the job. He left quickly and took all his plans with him.

No one except Banneker knew what to do. He had an amazing memory. He sat down and redrew the plans, right down to the last detail.

Presidents by the Numbers

8 Eight Presidents were born British subjects: Washington, Adams, Jefferson, Madison, Monroe, J. Q. Adams, Jackson, and W. Harrison.

9 Nine Presidents never attended college: Washington, Jackson, Van Buren, Taylor, Fillmore, Lincoln, A. Johnson, Cleveland, and Truman.

14 Fourteen Presidents served as vice presidents: J. Adams, Jefferson, Van Buren, Tyler, Fillmore, A. Johnson, Arthur, T. Roosevelt, Coolidge, Truman, Nixon, L. Johnson, Ford, and George H. W. Bush.

12 Vice presidents were originally the presidential candidates receiving the second-most electoral votes. The 12th Amendment, passed in 1804, changed the system so that the electoral college voted separately for President and vice president. Over time, the presidential candidate gained power to choose a running mate, but electoral votes are still cast separately.

2 For two years the nation was run by a President and a vice president who were not elected by the people: President Ford and Vice President Rockefeller in 1974–1976.

4 Four Presidents won the presidency but lost the popular vote: Andrew Jackson won the popular vote but lost the election to John Quincy Adams (1824); Samuel Tilden won the popular vote but lost the election to Rutherford B. Hayes (1876); Grover Cleveland won the popular vote but lost the election to Benjamin Harrison (1888); Al Gore won the popular vote but lost the election to George W. Bush (2000).

$400,000 The salary of the current President is $400,000. Washington's salary as President was $25,000, or about $250,000 in today's currency.

7 Only seven nationalities represent the heritage of all forty-three Presidents: Dutch, English, Irish, Scottish, Welsh, Swiss, and German.

1 There has been only one President who never married: Buchanan.

5'4" The shortest President was Madison.

6'4" The tallest President was Lincoln.

INDEX

A

Aaron, Henry (Hank), 48
abolitionists, 23
Adams, Abigail, 10, 56, 58
Adams, John, **10**, 56, 58, 62, 66
Adams, John Quincy, **14**, 15, 58, 66
Adams, Louisa, 58
Adu, Freddy, 55
Afghanistan, 52
African Americans
　citizenship granted to, 26
　civil rights of, 43, 45, 46
　education of, 28, 44
　segregation of, 44
Agnew, Spiro T., 47, 48, 61
Alaska, 26
Albright, Madeleine, 52
Al Qaeda, 55
ambulance, 33
American Red Cross, 29
Armstrong, Louis, 37
Armstrong, Neil, 47
Arthur, Chester A., 1, **30**, 60, 66
Arthur, Ellen, 60
Articles of Confederation, 4
atomic bomb, 43
Austria, 37, 40
automobiles, 33, 34

B

Bacon, Henry, 65
Bank of the United States, 16
Banneker, Benjamin, 65
Barkley, Alben W., 61
Barton, Clara, 29
baseball, 19, 28, 36, 48, 52
Bassett, Ebenezer, 26
Beatles, 46
Beethoven, Ludwig von, 11
Bell, Alexander Graham, 29
bicentennial, 48
Bill of Rights, 8
Billy the Kid, 29
Blackwell, Elizabeth, 20
Bolívar, Simón, 13
Booth, John Wilkes, 25
Bosnia, 53
Boy Scouts, 35
Braille, Louis, 14
Breckinridge, John C., 59
bribes, 37
Buchanan, James, **23**, 59, 66
Burr, Aaron, 58
Bush, Barbara, 57, 61
Bush, George H. W., **51**, 53, 54, 61, 66
Bush, George W., 51, **54–55**, 61, 66

Bush, Jeb, 51, 54
Bush, Laura, 57, 61
Bush, Prescott, 54
business
　regulation of, 35
　support of, 37, 38
Byrd, Robert E., 42

C

Cabinet, 6, 7
Calhoun, John C., 58, 59
California, 19, 20, 21, 36
Camp David peace agreement, 49
Carter, Jimmy, **49**, 50, 61
Carter, Rosalynn, 49, 57, 61
Castle-Hughes, Keisha, 54
Central Intelligence Agency (CIA), 51
Challenger space shuttle, 50
Cheney, Richard, 61
Cherokees, 16
Chile, 32
China, 33, 47, 48, 51, 53
Churchill, Winston, 41
Civil Rights Act, 46
Civil War
　battles, 25, 27
　Confederacy, 18, 23, 24–25
　slavery and, 24–25
Clark, William, 11
Clay, Henry, 21
Cleveland, Frances, 60
Cleveland, Grover, 1, **31**, 32, 60, 66
Clinton, George, 58
Clinton, Hillary Rodham, 52, 53, 57, 61
Clinton, William J., 1, **52–53**, 61
cold war, 43, 48, 50, 51
Colfax, Schuyler, 59
Columbia space shuttle, 50, 54
communism, 43
compact disk (CD), 47
Compromise of 1850, 21
Confederate Congress, 18
Confederate flag, 53
Confederate States of America, 18, 23, 24–25
Congress, 7, 65
Congressmen and women, 7
Constitution
　amendments to, 8, 26
　Bill of Rights, 8
　writing of, 12
Constitutional Convention, 4
Continental Congress, 8, 10
Coolidge, Calvin, **38**, 60, 66
Coolidge, Grace, 60
cotton gin, 9
court system, 6–7
　Supreme Court, 6–7, 8, 35, 44, 54

Crimean War, 22
Crippen, Bob, 50
Cuba, 33, 45
Curtis, Charles, 60
Custer, George, 27
Czolgosz, Leon, 33

D

Dallas, George M., 59
Davis, Jefferson, 23
Dawes, Charles G., 60
death penalty, 28
Declaration of Independence, 8, 10, 11, 32
delegates, 4
Democratic Party, 15, 22, 31, 44, 55
Dickens, Charles, 18
donkey symbol, 15
Douglas, Stephen A., 24
Dust Bowl, 40

E

Eastern Europe, 43
economy
　business, 35, 37, 38
　decline in, 48
　depression of 1848, 16
　employment, 41
　energy crisis, 49
　Great Depression, 38, 39, 40–41
　Great Panic of 1893, 31
　taxation, 41, 50, 51, 53, 55
　"trickle-down" theory, 50
Edison, Thomas, 28
education, 28, 44, 55
Egypt, 49
Eiffel Tower, 32
Eisenhower, Dwight D., 39, **44**, 47, 61
Eisenhower, Marie (Mamie), 61
electoral college, 5
electoral votes, 5, 14
Ellis Island, 32
Emancipation Proclamation, 24, 25
employment, 41
energy crisis, 49
Estonia, 51
ether, 18
euro, 53
executive branch, 6–7

F

Fairbanks, Charles W., 60
Fair Deal, 43
federal budget, 53
Fillmore, Abigail Powers, 21, 59
Fillmore, Millard, 1, **21**, 59, 66
First Ladies, 56–67

Fleming, Alexander, 38
Florida, 13
Folsom, Frances, 31
Ford, Betty, 48, 57, 61
Ford, Gerald R., **48**, 61, 66
Ford Motor Co., 34
Fort Sumter, 24
Fourteen Points, 36
France, 41, 43
Frank, Anne, 42
Franklin, Benjamin, 11
French Revolution, 8
Fulton, Robert, 11

G

Gagarin, Yuri, 45
Galveston flood, 33
Garfield, James A., **29**, 30, 60
Garfield, Lucretia, 60
Garner, John, 61
George III, King, 8
Germany, 36, 37, 40, 41, 42, 51
Gerry, Elbridge, 58
G.I. Bill, 43
gold, 19
Gold Rush, 20
Gorbachev, Mikhail, 50
Gore, Al, Jr., 53, 54, 61, 66
Grant, Julia, 59
Grant, Ulysses S., 25, **27**, 28, 59
Great Depression, 38, 39, 40–41
Great Panic of 1893, 31
Great Society, 46
Guam, 33
Guiteau, Charles J., 29

H

Habitat for Humanity, 49
Haiti, 11, 26
Hamilton, Alexander, 9
Hamlin, Hannibal, 59
Harding, Florence (Flossie), 37, 60
Harding, Warren G., 35, **37**, 38, 39
Harrison, Anna Tuthill, 59
Harrison, Benjamin, **32**, 60, 66
Harrison, Caroline, 60
Harrison, William Henry, **17**, 18, 31, 59, 66
Harry Potter and the Sorcerer's Stone, 53
Hawaii, 44
Hayes, Lucy, 28, 56, 60
Hayes, Rutherford B., **28**, 33, 56, 60, 66, 70
Head Start, 46
health care, 53
heart transplant, 46
Hendricks, Thomas, 60
Henson, Matthew, 34
Herschel, William, 28
Hoban, James, 62
Hobart, Garret, 60

Hoover, Herbert, **39**, 60
Hoover, Lou, 60
House of Representatives, 7
Hughes, Howard, 40
Humphrey, Hubert H., 61
Huygens space probe, 55

I

immigration, 30, 32
impeachment, 26, 47, 49
Indian Removal Act, 15
Indonesia, 43
Internet, 54
Iran hostage crisis, 49, 50
Iraq
    Desert Storm, 51
    U.S. invasion of, 55
Ireland, 19
Israel, 49
Italy, 40, 41

J

Jackson, Andrew, 14, **15**, 16, 59, 66
Japan, 41, 42–43
Jaws, 48
Jefferson, Martha, 58
Jefferson, Thomas, 9, 10, **11**, 13, 58, 64, 66
Jefferson Memorial, 64
Jews, 40
Johnson, Andrew, **26**, 59, 66
Johnson, Eliza, 59
Johnson, Lady Bird, 57, 61
Johnson, Lyndon B., 1, **46**, 61, 66
Johnson, Richard M., 59
Jordan, Michael, 53
judicial branch, 6–7

K

Kansas, 22, 23
Kansas-Nebraska Act, 22
Kennedy, Jacqueline, 45, 57, 61
Kennedy, John F., **45**, 46, 47, 52, 57, 61, 70
Kennedy, Robert, 46
Kentucky, 29
Key, Francis Scott, 12
King, Martin Luther, Jr., 45, 46
King, William R., 22, 59
Knox, Henry, 9
Korean War, 43, 44
Kosovo, 49
Kuwait, 51

L

Laden, Osama bin, 55
Latvia, 51
laws, 7
League of Nations, 36
Lee, Henry, 9

Lee, Robert E., 25, 27
legislation, 7
legislative branch, 6–7
L'Enfant, Pierre, 65
Lewis, Meriwether, 11
Lincoln, Abraham, 23, **24–25**, 26, 27, 59, 65, 66
Lincoln, Mary Todd, 25, 59
Lincoln Memorial, 65
Lindbergh, Charles, 38
Lithuania, 51
Little League, 48
Louisiana Purchase, 11, 13

M

Madison, Dolley, 56, 58
Madison, James, 1, **12**, 56, 58, 66
Maine, 13
Maine, battleship, 33
Mandela, Nelson, 51, 52
Marshall, Thomas R., 60
Marshall, Thurgood, 46
McCarthy Era, 47
McKinley, Ida, 60
McKinley, William, **33**, 34, 60
Medicare/Medicaid, 46
metric system, 9
Mexico, 13, 15, 19, 20, 36
Middle East, 49, 53
minimum wage, 44
Missouri Compromise, 13, 22
Mondale, Walter F., 61
Monroe, Elizabeth, 58
Monroe, James, **13**, 14, 58, 66
Monroe Doctrine, 13
moon landing, 47
Morse, Samuel, 18
Morton, Levi P., 60
motion pictures, 31

N

Napoleon, 10, 12
national parks, 27
Native Americans, 15, 16, 17, 20, 27, 32
Nazi Germany, 41
Nebraska, 22
New Deal, 41
New Mexico, 20
newspapers, 14
Nightingale, Florence, 22
Nixon, Richard M., 45, **47**, 48, 61, 66, 70
Nixon, Thelma (Pat), 47, 61
North Korea, 43
nuclear weapons, 50

O

oil wells, 23
Oklahoma City bombing, 52
Olympics, 49, 50
Oregon, 19

overrides, 7
Owens, Jesse, 40

P

Panama Canal, 34, 36
Pan-American Conference, 32
Parks, Rosa, 44
Peace Corps, 45
Peary, Robert E., 34
Perry, Matthew, 21
Philippine Islands, 33
Pierce, Franklin, **22**, 59
Pierce, Jane, 22, 59
Pluto, 39
Poe, Edgar Allan, 19
Polk, James K., **19**, 59
Polk, Sarah, 59
population, U.S., 8, 17, 20, 30, 43
postal routes, 30
poverty, 38, 46
Powell, Colin, 54
presidency, 4–5
Puerto Rico, 33

Q

Quayle, J. Danforth, 61

R

railroads, 13, 14, 15, 27, 31
Randolph, Edmund, 9
Reagan, Jane, 61
Reagan, Nancy, 61
Reagan, Ronald W., **50**, 51, 61, 70
Reconstruction, 26, 28
reelection, 5
Republican Party, 26, 30, 37, 44, 55
Rice, Condoleezza, 54
Rin Tin Tin, 37
Roaring Twenties, 38
Robinson, Jackie, 42
Rockefeller, Nelson A., 61, 66
rollerblades, 49
Roosevelt, Edith, 34, 60
Roosevelt, Eleanor, 40, 57, 61
Roosevelt, Franklin D., **40–41**, 42, 57, 61, 64
Roosevelt, Theodore, **34**, 35, 45, 60, 66, 70
Ross, James, 17
Ross, Nellie Tayloe, 38
Rough Riders, 34
Russia, 26, 49
Ruth, Babe, 36, 38

S

Sax, Adolphe, 17
Scott, Dred, 23
Senate, 7
September 11, 2001, terrorist attacks, 54, 55

Sherman, James S., 60
Sherman Antitrust Act, 32
Sioux Indians, 27
Sitting Bull, 27
slavery
    abolitionists, 23
    Amistad slave ship, 16
    Civil War and, 24–25
    in French colonies, 9
    prohibited, 26
    slave population, 20
    slaves as property, 23
    slave states, 13, 20, 22, 24
Smithsonian Institution, 14
soccer, 53, 55
South Africa, 51, 52
southern states, 20, 28
South Korea, 43
Soviet Union, 43, 45, 47, 49, 50, 51
space program, 45, 47, 50, 54, 55
Spanish-American War, 33
spoils system, 29, 30
Stalin, Joseph, 41
"Star-Spangled Banner, The," 12, 39
Statue of Liberty, 31
Stevenson, Adlai, 60
stock market crash, 39
Stowe, Harriet Beecher, 21
strikes, 31, 35
subways, 33

T

Taft, Helen (Nellie), 35, 60
Taft, William H., **35**, 60
Taliban, 52
taxation, 41, 50, 51, 53, 55
Taylor, Margaret, 59
Taylor, Zachary, **20**, 59, 66, 70
Tchaikovsky, 28
Teapot Dome Scandal, 37
teddy bear, 34
telegraph, 23
terrorism, 52, 54, 55
Texas, 15, 18, 19, 33, 36
Thoreau, Henry David, 22
Tiananmen Square rally, 51
Tilden, Samuel, 28, 66
Titanic, 35
Tompkins, Daniel D., 58
Trail of Tears, 16
Truman, Elizabeth (Bess), 61
Truman, Harry S., 39, **42–43**, 61, 66
tsunami, 55
TV, 43, 54
Twain, Mark, 27
Tyler, John, 17, **18**, 59, 66
Tyler, Julia, 59
Tyler, Letitia, 59

U

unemployment, 41

United Kingdom, 10
United Nations, 42
U.S. Capitol, 6–7, 10, 65
U.S. Department of Energy, 49
U.S. Supreme Court, 6–7, 8, 35, 44, 54, 64

V

Van Buren, Hannah, 59
Van Buren, Martin, 15, **16**, 17, 59, 66, 70
vetos, 7
Vice President, 6
Victoria, Queen, 16
Vietnam, 43
Vietnam War, 46, 47
voting
    by African Americans, 46
    electoral votes, 5, 14
    on legislation, 7
    by women, 31, 36
Voting Rights Act, 46

W

Wallace, Henry, 61
War of 1812, 12, 15, 17, 20
War on Poverty, 46
Washington, Booker T., 29
Washington, George, 1, 4, 5, **8–9**, 11, 56, 58, 66
Washington, Martha, 9, 56, 58
Washington Monument, 30, 65
Watergate scandal, 47
Wheeler, William A., 60
Whig Party, 18, 21
White House, 6–7, 62–63
Whitney, Eli, 9
Wilson, Edith, 56, 60
Wilson, Ellen, 60
Wilson, Henry, 59
Wilson, Woodrow, **36**, 37, 56, 60, 70
Wizard of Oz, The, 41
women's right to vote, 31, 36
World War I, 36, 37, 39, 42
World War II, 41, 42–43, 44, 45, 51
Wounded Knee, battle of, 32
Wright, Orville and Wilbur, 34

X

XYZ Affair, 10

Y

Yellowstone National Park, 27
Yeltsen, Boris, 49
Young, John, 50

In Their Own Words

"As to the presidency, the two happiest days of my life were those of my entrance upon the office and my surrender of it."
—Martin Van Buren

"Ask not what your country can do for you; ask what you can do for your country."
—John F. Kennedy

"Nothing brings out the lower traits of human nature like office seeking."
—Rutherford B. Hayes

"The idea that I should become President … has never entered my head, nor is it likely to enter the head of any other person."
—Zachary Taylor

"If you want to make enemies, try to change something."
—Woodrow Wilson

"I like the job I have, but if I had to live my life over again, I would like to have ended up a sportswriter."
—Richard M. Nixon

"America is too great for small dreams."
—Ronald W. Reagan

"Speak softly and carry a big stick."
—Theodore Roosevelt